FOR MY
ANGEL

FOR MY ANGEL

A TRUE STORY OF FORBIDDEN LOVE, OBSESSION, AND MURDER

BY

LINDA SASLOW

Doubleday Book & Music Clubs, Inc.

Garden City, New York

Book Design by Robert Aulicino

GuildAmerica Books™ is a trademark registration pending on
behalf of Doubleday Book & Music Clubs, Inc.

To my loving and supportive husband Jerry, and my two wonderful children, Julie and Craig, who encouraged and inspired me to turn my dream into a reality.
This book is for you.

Author's Note

This story is a reconstruction of actual events. Much of the dialogue in the book is taken from court transcripts and other recorded notes. But there are numerous instances in which the actual dialogue was unattainable, and therefore conversations and scenes have been re-created on the basis of interviews between the author and different individuals, in order to present more effectively the events that occurred.

In the instances for which there was more than one version of what happened, the material presented in this book is, in the author's judgment, the most plausible account, based on many hours of investigative interviews.

In order to protect the privacy of the many individuals interviewed, all names—aside from Oliver Petrovich, his parents Anna and Svetozar Petrovich, Oliver's girlfriend Karlene Francis, the defense and prosecuting attorneys during the trial, Nicholas A. Marino and Daniel Cotter respectively, presiding judge John S. Thorp, Jr., Alan Klein, board-certified clinical psychologist and witness for the defense, Roger Feldman, licensed physician, practicing psychiatrist, and witness for the defense, Nassau County homicide detectives Brian Parpan and Vincent Donnelly—have been changed, as well as the address of the Petrovich home. Any similarity to actual people, living or dead, is purely coincidental.

PROLOGUE:
September 24, 1988

Betrayed by his own mother.

Oliver felt the muscles in his stomach tighten and his hands begin to tremble.

How could she have done this to him? Their secret arrangement had been working out so well, and she had to ruin it all by telling his father.

Now he'd lose his Angel.

Clenching his hands together to stop them from shaking, he began to pace.

No one could take away his Angel. Who would take care of her? She needed him. And he needed her. He'd do anything for his Angel.

His heart was racing as it battled against his mind. The war inside him was escalating and the anxiety within him was mounting so fast that he felt dizzy.

He looked across the table at the traitor, and barely

recognized his own mother. She was the obstacle to his happiness. They both were. They'd have to be removed. There was no choice.

In a sudden motion he put his arm around her throat and squeezed.

They both fell to the ground. When he let go of her throat she started screaming.

He reached for the shotgun he had left under the kitchen table. He saw that she was trying to stand up. He had no time to lose. He aimed at the back of her head and shot her.

The moment she fell, a pool of blood began forming around her.

His job was half done.

Minutes later, his obstacles to happiness with Angel were eliminated: both his parents lay dead.

Chapter 1: APRIL 1988:

"MY LITTLE ANGEL"

Oliver Petrovich was cruising the New Rochelle mall on a Sunday in April when he first met Karlene Francis. On a lunch break from her job as cashier at Everyone's, a beauty supply shop, she was sitting alone at a small table in the corner of the mall's food court, picking at a cheeseburger in front of her.

From the end of the line at the nearby hamburger stand, Oliver noticed her skin, the rich color of cocoa, and was immediately struck by her beauty. He watched her eating and was suddenly compelled to go over and meet her.

He shuffled restlessly in his place, willing the line to

move faster so he could get his burger before she finished her meal.

He leaned over to get a better look at her table, trying to find out if there was more than one tray on it. When he saw only one, he was relieved that she was by herself.

Oliver knew he was being obvious but he didn't care. He continued to stare at her.

He tried to lock eyes with her, hoping for even a faint smile. But when she noticed him watching her and met his eyes, she quickly looked away.

Captured by her face, he couldn't look away. She had the flawless features of a woman, yet in her eyes there was a lost expression that made her seem more like a child.

He could see that she was thin, almost painfully so. But at the same time there was a sensuality about her that held his fascination.

She was wearing white silky pants with a matching white blouse, from which her brown arms extended gracefully. They looked like velvet; Oliver longed to touch them.

The voice of the teenager behind the fast-food counter summoned Oliver's attention as he realized that he had reached the front of the line.

"May I help you?" the boy asked in a voice that sounded as if it still hadn't completed the change from the high squeak of puberty.

"Burger, small f-fries, and a large Coke."

Relieved that he had barely stuttered, Oliver wasted no time in finding napkins or a straw, but took his tray and hurried toward her table.

She had finished eating and was assembling the Styrofoam container and the soda cup on her tray, preparing to leave.

Instinctively he grabbed her arm, and in a voice gruffer than he meant asked, "What's your name?"

"I don't have a name." She looked annoyed and pushed his arm off hers.

He slid into the empty seat next to her and tried again to catch her eyes. "Maybe we could get together and go to a movie?"

She started to get up, and finally looked at him. "You're really strange. I wouldn't go out with you."

"Come on," he persisted. "I'm not really strange."

She picked up her tray to leave. "I've got to get back to work."

"Then how about giving me your phone number and I'll call you and maybe we can go out?"

In a sudden and unexpected motion, she put her tray down and picked up an unused napkin. Reaching into her handbag, she pulled out a pen and carefully wrote down a name and phone number on the paper napkin. "You really are a strange guy," she repeated. As she handed the paper to Oliver she smiled for the first time. "I really have to go."

As Oliver continued to watch her, his first impression was confirmed. She definitely was too skinny, but still had a great body.

He knew that she could have given him a phony name and phone number. But with the possibility of seeing her again, Oliver felt like singing.

At home that evening he unfolded the napkin from his pocket and read the name: Karlene Francis. Maybe the name on the paper was a fake, but it was a nice name anyway, he thought.

He dialed the numbers from the napkin on the

kitchen phone while his mother was washing the dinner dishes.

"Who are you calling, Olly?" she asked innocently while drying a pot.

"Some girl I met at a mall," he answered nonchalantly.

"Nice girl?" She always liked to make idle chatter while she put the dishes away.

"Yeah, Ma; she's a nice girl."

Oliver chuckled to himself. What would his mother say if he added, "A nice black girl, Ma."

That one word would change everything for his parents, he knew, because they were racists. They hated blacks—especially ones he might date. And after his fling with Wendy, his last black girlfriend, they were bigger racists than ever. Perfect candidates for the KKK, he thought. His mother was bad, but his father was even worse.

Someone answered on the other end of the phone. He recognized her voice instantly. Was he dreaming, or had she actually given him her real name and phone number?

"Hi, uh, K-Karlene? This is Oliver Petrovich." He stopped to catch his breath. "I met you in the mall today. Remember m-m-me?"

"Yeah," she answered. He had to strain to hear her.

"G-good." He struggled to get the words out. Caught unprepared, he was trying frantically to regain his cool. "So, uh, do you want to go out with me?"

"When?"

"How about tomorrow?"

"Yeah, okay."

"Okay, great. So I'll pick you up after work, okay? About seven o'clock?"

"Okay."

He grabbed a nearby pencil and scribbled down the New Rochelle address she gave him over the phone. After a brief hesitation he heard her voice again.

"Oliver?"

"Yeah?"

"Make sure you show up on time."

Ten minutes after he hung up the phone, Oliver was still whistling.

If there had been a way to make the clock move faster, Oliver would have figured it out. The hours at the Pepsi-Cola plant, where he worked as a truck mechanic helper, dragged on.

All day he wondered how long it would take him to get from Mount Vernon to New Rochelle. He worried if he'd be able to find her house, if she remembered what he looked like, if she was serious about the date or just playing a joke on him. And he tried to remember where there was a flower store near work.

When the six o'clock buzzer sounded he punched his card out, ran to his car, and sped out of the parking lot. Consumed with getting there on time, he didn't bother to change his clothes but kept on the same brown baggy slacks and tan Mickey Mouse T-shirt that he had worn all day.

But by the time he finally found a florist it was closed, then he got lost trying to find her street, and Oliver arrived at Karlene's front door a half hour late.

She was home alone.

"Do you always let s-strangers in your house?" he teased.

"Not really." She moved gracefully and looked even

more beautiful than he remembered from the day before. But Oliver thought that she seemed nervous.

He followed her into the kitchen, where they both stood awkwardly facing each other.

"Hey, we don't have to stay here," he offered. "Maybe your p-p-parents would be angry that you're home alone with a guy."

She answered softly. "I don't live with my parents."

"Then who—"

"Mary. A woman who rents me a room here. I moved out of my house when I was fifteen."

She looked down at her long red fingernails. There again was a silence between them, until Oliver broke the spell.

"Let's get out of here. Let's go sit in my car. We can talk b-better there and we can go for a r-ride."

She hesitated, then followed him toward the front door.

As she locked the house, Oliver turned again to look at her. She had on a pair of tight black jeans and the same white blouse she had been wearing the day before. In her heels, she was about the same height he was, so he figured that in her bare feet she was probably about five feet nine, only about an inch shorter than his five ten. And she couldn't weigh more than a hundred pounds. He'd have to fatten her up, he thought as he put his hand on her shoulder.

Karlene Francis. He said her name to himself. He was still surprised that she had given him her real phone number.

When she saw his maroon four-door 1985 Plymouth Fury parked outside of the house, she smiled.

"This is my baby," he said lovingly as he opened the

door for her. "It was an unmarked p-police car b-before I bought it and fixed it up."

"I can tell; it still looks like one," she answered.

Oliver started the car and began to drive slowly down the street. Neither spoke for several blocks.

Oliver was trying to think of what he could talk about to make it easier for her, but his mind was blank.

"Do you want to go to a m-movie?" he tried.

"No."

"Hey, come on, I think there are a few good movies playing on Francis Lewis Boulevard. Let's check it out."

He interpreted her silence as agreement and put on the radio to distract from their clumsy attempts at conversation.

By the time they arrived at the theater they had just missed all of the eight o'clock movies, and there were two hours before any of the next showings was scheduled to start.

Oliver bought tickets for the earliest one, which sounded like a horror film, even though he had never heard of it.

The sun had gone down and the temperature had dropped sharply. Both in short sleeves, they had goose bumps on their arms from the cool evening air of early spring. Oliver turned on the heat in the car.

With time to kill and awkwardness between them, he sensed her uneasiness and he too began to feel tense.

"Listen, relax, it's okay." He spoke gently. "I'm not g-g-going to hurt you."

She smiled nervously.

"Are you hungry?" At least getting a bite to eat would give them something to do, he thought.

"I guess." Her voice was barely louder than a whisper.

Oliver turned the radio louder and drove to a nearby Jacks, a hamburger joint, where he ordered burgers and shakes for the car.

Slowly, as they started eating, they both began to relax. Curiosity soon overcame their shyness as the two strangers tried to learn something about each other.

"So how old are you, anyway?" he asked.

"Nineteen," she answered, adding quickly, "I've been on my own for the last four years."

"Why?" he wondered out loud. "Why did you leave home?"

Her jaw tightened and the expression on her face turned suddenly angry. "I couldn't live with my mother. I couldn't take her shit anymore."

"So where'd you go?"

"First to a group home. Then a foster home. Then this apartment. But . . ." She looked away.

"But what?"

"Mary's boyfriend was always trying to fool around with me. And then—" Her voice was beginning to quiver. "Then he raped me." She stopped and took a deep breath before continuing. "But when I told Mary she called me a liar and kicked me out. So I lost my home."

"So then what?" Oliver watched as she looked down at the pocketbook on her lap and played absently with the snap. "So my uncle said I could live with him for a while, even though I knew he really didn't want me. But I had nowhere else to go, so I moved in with him. And then a few months ago Mary came to my uncle's and told me I could come back. That she believed me. Finally. Big deal, right? Finally she believed I was telling the truth."

The tears were rolling down her cheeks as she continued softly. "She said that she'd kicked her boyfriend out and he wouldn't bother me anymore." Karlene pulled a tissue out of her bag and wiped her eyes. "What a joke, right? She only wanted me back because she needs the money I pay her for rent. But the biggest joke is that I went back, because I knew my uncle wanted to get rid of me and I didn't know where else to go." She wiped a few stray tears with her hand. "God only knows where I'll be living next year." Looking at Oliver, she forced a smile. "So now it's your turn. What about you?"

In few words he told her that he was twenty-three, a truck mechanic, an only child, and a car fanatic. His parents had come over from Yugoslavia before he was born. He said he was born at Saint Clare's Hospital and grew up in Manhattan where his family lived until 1984, when his father had bought a house on Long Island, in Great Neck.

"Want to see our house?" he suggested. "We're not far, and we still have time to kill before the movie starts."

"Okay," she agreed softly.

When they pulled up to the house at 64 Richard Avenue, Oliver parked his car on the street, and with his finger to his lips motioned for Karlene to follow him silently.

Using his key, he opened the front door and, hearing his parents' voices back in the kitchen, called out,

"Hi, Ma, I'm home. I'm going upstairs. Good night. See you in the morning."

Following his lead, Karlene tiptoed into the house and across the hall toward the staircase leading to his bedroom.

Only when they were safely upstairs in his bedroom did either of them finally speak. And even with the door closed and locked, they both whispered.

"Why did we have to sneak in here like that?" she asked. With wide eyes, she was looking all around his room. Oliver thought she resembled a cat, checking out unfamiliar territory.

"You don't know my parents. They wouldn't understand." He walked over to his dresser and turned the stereo on low.

"Understand what?" She had a blank expression on her face.

"Well, the best way to put it is that they're racists."

"What's that supposed to mean?"

"It m-m-means that they hate blacks and don't want m-me hanging out, or going out, with any."

"Oh, I see." Still standing, she turned to face away from him and walked toward the window.

He followed her, put his arm on her shoulder and tried to turn her around to kiss her.

But she backed away and turned her face so as not to meet his eyes.

Oliver stood motionless, with an expression that a young boy might have after being scolded by his teacher.

Karlene caught sight of his face, and suddenly started to laugh. She turned to face him and slowly walked closer until they were touching.

She put her hands on his face and kissed him softly on the lips.

Oliver wrapped his arms around her and drew her to him, kissing her harder, while urgently he began to pull off her clothes, and then his own.

Once they were both naked he drew her onto his double bed and, never letting his mouth leave hers, began to move his hands over her body. Without clothes she was even more exquisite than he had imagined, her skin even softer than he had fantasized.

In bed Karlene lost her shyness. She responded to his caresses with a passion that surprised and excited him. For more than an hour they explored each other. When he touched secret parts of her she moaned softly, which added even further to his pleasure.

After they had finished making love, satisfied and exhausted, they lay naked together under Oliver's sheets, her head resting on his chest, his arms wrapped gently around her while he gazed down at her.

This time it was she who broke the silence first. "You're so serious, Oliver. Why do you keep staring at me?"

"Because you're very beautiful." He tightened his arms around her.

"But don't you ever smile?"

"Sure. When there's something to s-smile about."

She looked up into his eyes and softly kissed his lips. "Is this something to smile about?"

Oliver smiled.

"So you can smile," she teased. "And you have such a beautiful smile. You should try it more often."

He kissed her forehead. "You're so sweet and beautiful, you're like a little angel." He took her chin in his hand. "My angel." Once again, he smiled. "I think from now on I'll call you Angel."

Oliver and Angel never made it to the movies that evening. Familiar with the predictable patterns of his parents, he knew they'd never come upstairs and he insisted that Karlene spend the night with him.

Again and again they made love—softly, urgently, passionately.

Realizing that he had to go to work the next morning and couldn't be late, Oliver figured that if they left early enough they could sneak out of the house before his parents were awake. As planned, they woke and dressed silently and tiptoed downstairs. They were at the front door when Oliver's father suddenly appeared.

Svetozar Petrovich, a burly man of fifty-nine with a heavy Yugoslavian accent, stared at his son and the black girl in front of him.

Without a word, Oliver guided Karlene out of the house and toward his car.

Svetozar shouted after him, "Who is this bitch, Oliver? I'm warning you, the next time I see her, I'll shoot her!"

Then Oliver and the girl were gone.

That evening Oliver and Karlene went to see the horror movie they had missed the night before. When Oliver told the manager they had gotten stuck with a flat tire, he let them in with their old tickets.

No longer could a day pass when Oliver didn't see his Angel. She was on his mind every waking minute. He counted the hours at work until he could see her, touch her, hold her, love her. For two weeks he sneaked her up to his room at every possible opportunity. Finally he suggested that she move in with him. It would be simple, he figured. She could live upstairs in his room, and if they heard either of his parents coming up, she'd hide in his closet.

They quickly discovered that they could avoid Oliver's father, but it was impossible to hide from his mother who was always home.

Anna Petrovich, fifteen years younger than her husband and more modern in her thinking, agreed to keep their secret; Oliver and Angel shared the ecstasy of relief.

Until the one night, six months later, that Anna Petrovich would suddenly change her mind and tell her husband that a nigger girl had been living with Oliver in his room.

And it would be that very same night, just a few hours after the secret was out, that Oliver Petrovich would murder both his parents.

Chapter 2:
JANUARY 1972:
"HAPPY BIRTHDAY, OLIVER"

As he blew out the candles on his cake, Oliver didn't feel any older but he knew that the family celebration was in honor of his seventh birthday. The Christmas tree was still up and the apartment had a lingering air of festivity. His Aunt Rosa and Uncle George had been invited to dinner with his two cousins, and Oliver had permission to stay up late on a Saturday night. His mother had even cooked a spicy meatball dish that she said was a Yugoslavian specialty and his father had bought his favorite whipped cream cake with pineapple filling and "Happy Birthday Oliver" written in large script blue letters.

But the best part of this birthday was that it meant that Oliver was finally getting the two-wheeler bike that he had been dreaming about since his parents promised it to him almost a year ago.

"I can't believe my baby is seven." Anna Petrovich stood behind Oliver's chair at the dining room table, her eyes filled with tears as she watched him finish blowing out the last candle. She grabbed him from behind and hugged him tightly with her plump arms. "My baby," she repeated. "Where have the years gone?"

Even after living in New York for twelve years, his mother, unlike her husband, still spoke in a Yugoslavian dialect at home. Oliver's parents had both come to the United States in the early sixties, had met in Manhattan and gotten married. His mother had learned enough English to get by, but preferred speaking in her native tongue.

"Before we eat the cake, what do you say we get your birthday present?" she suggested in Yugoslavian, her eyes twinkling.

"Could we, Mommy?" Oliver responded in English as he bounded from his seat, beating his mother to the closet at the other end of the living room. His cousins followed on Oliver's heels, with their parents close behind.

"Okay, Oliver, stand here and close your eyes," she ordered playfully, then she opened the closet and wheeled out the new bike.

On command, Oliver opened his eyes to the shiniest, most beautiful bike he had ever seen. It had a black frame, a red seat, and taped to the handlebars was a giant red bow. It even had a horn and a siren, which he immediately tested.

"Do you like it, baby?" Anna put one hand on his shoulder, and with the other wiped away the tears that had again escaped from her eyes when she saw her son's look of joy and the radiant smile on his face.

"My boy, Olly," she repeated. "You're so beautiful when you smile." She looked into his deep brown eyes. "You're too serious, Oliver," she thought out loud. "You should smile more often."

"Oh Mommy, this is the best present. I love it. Thank you so much." His smile stretched from one end of his face to the other. He let go of the bike to hug his mother and was smothered in the warmth of her bosom. Then he turned back toward the dining room to look for his father, hoping for a kiss or a hug for his birthday.

Svetozar had risen from his seat at the dining room table and was walking slowly toward the group with his arms folded, his lips pursed, his face expressionless.

Oliver's father walked over to the bike and patted the seat. He looked at Oliver. "Quite a bike," he said, testing the horn. "Not bad, is it, son?"

Oliver felt his hopes for any affection from his father disintegrate in an instant. "It's g-great. Th-thank you." He looked down at the carpet in front of his father.

While his father continued to appraise the new bike from all angles, Oliver saw his Aunt Rosa pulling on his mother's arm to get her attention.

"Where did that stutter come from, Anna?" she whispered so loudly that everyone in the room could hear her. "Is this something new? I never noticed Oliver stuttering before. What's wrong with him?"

Speechless, Anna looked away from her sister-in-law and over toward her husband, waiting for him to react.

"It's nothing," Svetozar snapped. "Nothing to make a big deal over. Lots of kids stutter. And they outgrow it." He stormed out of the living room.

"It's nothing," Anna repeated softly, more to herself than to anyone in the room.

The tension in the room was quickly broken by Oliver's uncle, who had been quietly standing in front of the sofa and now walked over toward the three children.

"Okay, kids, go play in Oliver's room and let the grownups have a cup of coffee in peace." He patted Oliver's head. "Oliver, you take care of your cousins, okay, sport? We'll call you when it's time for the cake." He started toward the dining room, but turned back to his wife and his sister, still frozen in place. "Come on, Anna. I could sure go for a cup of your delicious coffee."

George went to join Svetozar at the dining room table, while the two women scurried into the kitchen to prepare coffee for their husbands.

Away from the grownups, Oliver felt his body relax. With his two younger cousins, who were five and six, he was in command.

"Come on, you shrimps," he ordered them. "Let's play cops and robbers."

The girls obediently followed him into his room and he closed the door. While they were looking inside his closet for the guns, Oliver moved slyly toward the light switch, and in one sudden motion flicked off the lights, leaving his room in total darkness.

Both girls screamed.

Within seconds Anna rushed into the room to find
out what had happened. But by the time she opened
the door Oliver had turned the lights back on and was
sitting nonchalantly at his desk reading an Archie
comic, a look of innocence on his face.

"Aunt Anna, Oliver is scaring us!" whined six-year-
old Terry. "He turned off the lights and we couldn't
see!"

"We were sooo scared!" echoed her five-year-old
sister Paula.

"It's okay, girls," Anna said gently. Then she looked
sternly at her son. "Oliver, that's not nice," she repri-
manded. "Don't do that again."

His mother turned to leave. "I'll leave the door open
so we can hear you." She turned back to look at the
three children. "Now play nice. We'll call you when
it's cake time."

As soon as his mother was gone, Oliver glared at his
two cousins. He scrunched up his face to scare them,
while pushing his two fingers inside his mouth and
stretching it from both ends.

"Tattletales, tattletales," he sang after he had pulled
his fingers out of his mouth. "Babies, babies, stick
your heads in gravy." As he continued teasing the girls
in his singsong voice, he smoothly backed toward his
door and in one move slammed the door shut and
again turned out the lights, this time making scary
ghost noises in the dark as the room turned to black-
ness.

"Mommy! Help!" Terry screamed.

"Aunt Anna! Oliver is scaring us!" Paula whined.

For the second time within minutes Oliver's mother
came to his room, but again, by the time she reached

the door the lights were on and Oliver was back in the same position, reading his comic book.

The girls were cowering together on Oliver's bed, and when Anna looked into the brightly lit room they both started to giggle nervously.

"That's enough, Oliver," his mother said, her tone sounding more tired than angry. "You're not behaving like the big boy that you're supposed to be now." She put her hands on his shoulders and shook them gently. "Come on, now. Be nice to your cousins." And she turned back to join the other adults.

Oliver walked over to his dresser and pulled something out of the bottom drawer, which he quickly hid under his shirt. "I'll be right back; I'm going to the bathroom," he informed the girls.

Less than a minute later, they heard his voice from down the hall. "Terry, come here. Quick."

Curious to see what he wanted, Terry bounded from Oliver's bed and was rounding the corner toward the bathroom when she was splashed in the face with cold water from a water gun.

"Gotcha!" her cousin taunted as he continued to squirt her.

Terry let out a shriek.

"You ninny," Oliver muttered. "Shhh." He put his finger to his lips. "Keep your voice down; we'll get in trouble."

It was too late. As Oliver turned to head back toward his room he heard the sound of adult footsteps approaching. His mother would really be angry this time, he thought. He'd have to make up a good story to placate her.

But as Oliver turned the bend, it was not his mother who was waiting for him but his father.

Svetozar grabbed Oliver by the shirt and pulled him roughly toward him. "I guess you didn't understand your mother!" he yelled at his son in Yugoslavian. "So I will have to explain it to you in a way that you're sure to understand!"

Keeping his hold on Oliver's shirt, his father dragged him down the hall and into the empty kitchen. He yanked a kitchen chair out from under the table and shoved Oliver toward it.

From experience, Oliver knew what he was expected to do. While his father tugged the belt from his pants, Oliver lay across the chair, his stomach on the vinyl seat, his head resting on his arms, preparing himself for the inevitable. At least his father hadn't made him take his pants off this time, he thought as he felt the belt whip across his bottom.

Oliver always promised himself that he wouldn't cry, but the sudden pain brought immediate tears to his eyes. He bit down hard on his fist, trying to regain self-control.

Svetozar Petrovich was not a tall man, but his stocky build gave the appearance of strength, the impression of power. Oliver knew that once his father raised the belt over him it was as if he were driven by another force that wouldn't let him stop. He'd often continue to beat Oliver until his concentration was distracted or he got tired.

"How do you like this?" his father shouted as he whipped his son. "Is it worth it to be disobedient and disrespectful?" He hit him again. "Don't you ever think you can get away with it!" he growled.

Oliver was spared tonight because there was company in the apartment, and after only a few lashes his father stopped. "Now get up!" Svetozar ordered. "And behave like the man you're supposed to be!"

Oliver straightened himself off the chair and stood before his father, his eyes cast down at the yellow linoleum floor.

"Look at me when I talk to you!" his father barked at him.

He slowly picked his head up to meet his father's eyes.

"Remember, Oliver, big boys must behave like big boys," his father said, his voice slowly beginning to lose its anger. "Now let's go into the dining room and have some of your birthday cake. Come on, put a smile on your face."

More than anything he could think of, Oliver wanted to please his father. He longed to gain his approval; then maybe his father would hug him and, just once, tell Oliver that he loved him. But as hard as he tried to force a smile, the leftover pain from his father's belt, combined with the humiliation of being whipped when they had company, brought only more tears.

Oliver slowly followed his father into the dining room, where he was greeted by a blur of faces plastered with awkward smiles.

"Come, darling," his mother coaxed. "Have some cake." She slid over a plate with a huge piece of his favorite pineapple-filled cake.

"Sit right here, my big seven-year-old," she said tenderly. As she gently reached over to push back a wisp of hair that had fallen in his face, she said softly, "Happy birthday, dear Oliver."

Chapter 3: APRIL 1988:
"INTO THE CLOSET!"

Oliver had never felt like this before. He thought about Angel from the minute he woke up, all day long, and until he crawled into bed at night. And even then he often dreamed about her.

Aside from his insatiable sexual hunger for her body, there was something so pitiful about her that sometimes Oliver only longed to wrap his strong arms around her, to hold her tight and promise her that nobody would ever hurt her again, that he'd always be there to protect her.

Many mornings before work he set his alarm for six o'clock and drove in rush-hour traffic for almost an hour to New Rochelle so he could take Angel to a nearby McDonald's, be sure she ate breakfast, and spend a little time with her before he dropped her off at the high school where she was working toward her diploma.

From the moment he watched her disappear behind the school doors, he started counting the hours until he would see her again. Even at work some of the other mechanics and truck drivers noticed a change in him.

"Hey, Petrovich, what gives?" one of the drivers teased him. "You're not giving us a hard time and being a jackass like usual." In fun, he rolled his eyeballs at Oliver. "Are you, like, in love, or something?"

Oliver continued working on the engine of one of the Pepsi trucks and answered, "Put it this way, Wilson. I found my Angel."

Every evening at exactly six o'clock Oliver made a beeline to his car and tore out of the Pepsi plant. He usually popped one of his favorite Rod Stewart tapes into the tape deck and blasted it on high volume as he sped up the Hutchinson River Parkway. Thinking about seeing Angel, he drove even faster—often up to 100 miles per hour. But Oliver knew that his Plymouth Fury still looked like an unmarked highway patrol car, and to make it look even more convincing he had bought the extra black door bumpers he had seen on other patrol cars.

He didn't worry about being picked up on radar because he knew that even if they were waiting for him, once they spotted his car they would be confused. With his short haircut and serious expression, Oliver could whiz by at such speed that the highway cops would assume he was one of them. On a few occasions police officers actually stuck out their hands to wave

hello as he sped past them. This made Oliver feel ter-
rific, since his long-time dream was to become a cop.
He had his own police manual at home, and was
studying to take the exam to become a police officer.

Once Angel was in the car, Oliver changed the music because he knew she preferred soft rock or romantic love songs. It didn't matter to him what music was
playing, as long as she was beside him.

Their favorite spot was a children's playground in
Flushing Meadow Park, not far from Oliver's house.
They often picked up Kentucky Fried Chicken or Mc-
Donald's for dinner and spent hours together side by
side on the swings, bouncing on the seesaw or just
sitting together on the grass overlooking a small lake.
They couldn't keep their hands off each other. After
dark, when they had the park to themselves, they
made love in Oliver's car or outside on the grass.

At their playground one clear spring night, near
midnight, they were both feeling unusually daring and
adventurous. They had just climbed through a children's maze which ended with a winding tube slide.
Still inside the slide together, they made love, giggling
with abandon like two little children. Afterward they
slid out the bottom of the tube and lay on the sand,
their arms wrapped around each other, looking up at
the sky and counting the stars.

As the weather grew warmer they drove around
searching for traveling carnivals that opened for a
week at a time in different towns. On those evenings
dinner often consisted of popcorn and cotton candy.
Hand in hand, Oliver and Karlene played the carnival
games and went on every ride until they had used up
all of the money Oliver had in his pocket or until the
carnival closed, whichever came first.

On other evenings they drove out to Jones Beach, on Long Island's south shore, where they walked along the sand, built giant sand castles, and made love right on the beach. On the warmer nights they waded in the ocean. When no one else was on the beach they stripped out of their clothes and lay naked together in the sand at the edge of the water, laughing as the tiny waves gently washed over their bodies before receding back into the ocean. They inched their way deeper into the water but Karlene was afraid of the ocean and wouldn't go past her knees unless Oliver took her in his arms and carried her out a little farther into the deeper water. As the waves rushed by them she clung to him fiercely, and he held her tenderly.

When it rained they went to a movie or to any of several nearby shopping malls and walked up and down the aisles, stopping often to look in store windows. If something caught Karlene's eye, Oliver immediately went inside and bought it for her. More than once Oliver spent his entire week's paycheck on his Angel within a few hours at a mall. He wanted her to look good and have beautiful things but paid no attention to his own appearance and usually dressed in the same baggy brown slacks and a faded T-shirt.

"Come on, Oliver," Karlene urged as they admired a window of a men's store. "At least buy yourself one nice shirt and a pair of slacks. You look like a slob."

"What for?" he answered, his attention already moving on to the next store.

"Because you dress like shit and you're so handsome. You should take better care of how you look." She gave him a playful shove.

"It's not important, Angel," he said, distracted by a car magazine that he had spotted by the entrance of a

card store. "I don't care about what I wear; I don't
have to look at m-myself." He put his arm around her
and drew her to him. "I'd rather l-look at you. And I
can't wait to see you in this hot outfit." He pointed to
the shopping bag she was carrying, filled with a white
cotton jumpsuit they had just bought at a small bou-
tique.

Oliver headed over to get a better look at the magazine. "Now this is what I care about," he said with
growing enthusiasm. "Check out the body on this machine."

"Oh, Oliver." Giving up on her attempt to improve
his wardrobe, Karlene nuzzled closer to him.

Whatever money from his paycheck that he didn't
spend on Angel, Oliver spent on his other love, his car
—for new parts and accessories. He bought every car
magazine as soon as it came out on the stand, and
often spent hours in automotive stores looking for one
tiny part and leaving with more than a hundred dollars' worth of merchandise.

"You're obsessed with your dumb car," Karlene
often complained.

"Yeah, but you still c-c-come first," he teased back.

Sometimes she got annoyed, especially when he
was with his best friend Danny and all the two of them
talked about was cars. But more often Karlene was
amused.

On Saturday nights they liked to pull over along
Francis Lewis Boulevard in Queens, to watch the hot-
rodders speeding by. Oliver laughed as many of them
slowed down when they saw his car, thinking it was a
police car. Several times a real highway patrol car
pulled up next to them and started talking to them,
figuring Oliver and Karlene for partners on the high-

way. When the police officers realized that they were just two young lovebirds, some were annoyed, others amused, but all left them alone and drove off. Afterward Oliver and Karlene would giggle all the way back to Great Neck.

If his father was already asleep when they got home, Oliver parked the car on the street out front and they tiptoed into the house together. But if they got home before his parents' bedtime Oliver often dropped Karlene off down the block and instructed her to walk the rest of the way so he could pull up to the house alone—just in case his father was watching. She'd wait by the side of the house until Oliver gave her the all-clear signal, and then they'd silently climb the stairs to his bedroom.

They could never get enough of each other. Karlene got used to sneaking in and out of Oliver's room, where they spent hours together exploring each other's bodies, kissing, experimenting with new love-making positions, and talking—always in whispers. Oliver often kept the stereo on to drown their voices.

"Oliver, your room is so disgustingly neat," Karlene remarked one night. "It looks like nobody lives here. Why don't you put up some posters or something?"

"I c-can't," he answered shortly.

"Why not?" she persisted.

"My f-f-father won't allow it." His voice was a mixture of fear and contempt. "He likes everything a certain way, and I have no say in his decisions."

In the room were a double bed with a small night table on each side, an antique dresser, a free-standing full-length mirror, and a comfortable chair, with a flat, faded Chinese area rug on the floor. The walls were bare except for one wooden carving of fruits, and only a stereo and small color TV decorated the top of Oliver's dresser.

The rest of the brick-and-cedar Cape Cod house at 64 Richard Avenue had the same feeling. With plastic runners over the carpets, several deer heads that his father had hunted, mounted on the walls of the living room, and nothing ever out of place, it looked more like a museum than a home. Even the garage was immaculate. Tools and equipment were kept in systematic order, and in a corner was a table for the vegetables grown in Anna Petrovich's garden; the lettuce, tomatoes, and zucchini were lined up in perfect rows.

It wasn't the kind of home Oliver or Karlene dreamed of for themselves. They were able to ignore its coldness because once behind the locked door of Oliver's room, they both felt safe and comfortable.

But the safety and comfort of their routine ended abruptly one evening in late April. After work, when Oliver picked Karlene up at the New Rochelle library, he could tell right away that something was wrong.

"What's the m-matter, Angel?" he asked, with concern in his voice.

"It's Mary, my landlord. She's giving me a real hard time." She sounded as nervous as she had the night of their first date.

"That bitch." Oliver felt the anger beginning to rise inside of him. "What did she d-do to you?"

"She's been noticing all the new things you've been buying me, Oliver," Karlene explained softly. "And she's been making comments." She mimicked her foster mother. "Nice shirt, Karlene. Nice pocketbook, Karlene. Is that new? Did you get that from your rich boyfriend?"

Looking down at her trembling hands, her voice

was also shaky. "So then the other day she said to me that she needs more money—that the eighty dollars a week I pay her isn't enough, and she wants one hundred and fifty." She paused and looked up at Oliver's face. "She wants me to make up the difference, and she told me to go ask my rich boyfriend for the money."

Oliver's fists were clenched as he listened to her and watched her troubled face. "So what did you tell her?" he asked, trying to control his anger.

"I told her to go fuck herself, and I bolted out of the house."

Later that night when Oliver took Karlene back to her rented home, they found that her room had been emptied of all her personal belongings and several small valises were waiting by the front door with a note taped to one that confirmed Karlene's worst fears: she had been kicked out.

"Oh, Oliver, what am I going to do now?" she cried, her voice bordering on hysteria.

"Relax, Angel." Oliver tried to comfort her and give her a sense of optimism that he himself didn't feel. "We'll f-figure something out."

Oliver's first plan was to bring Karlene back to her parents' house in White Plains. During the ride to her former home they tried to make each other believe that this would be the best place for her, and it would only be temporary.

But when they got to the house, Karlene's stepfather was the first to come to the door. And when he saw her valises his welcoming words to his stepdaughter were, "Karlene, when are you gonna stop this shit?"

From inside, Karlene's mother called to her, and mother and daughter disappeared into the house for a while. When Karlene returned outside she was crying. Between sobs her words could barely be understood. "They don't want me here, Oliver."

"Come on, Angel." He pulled her to him. "Let's get out of here. We'll f-find you a b-better home than this heartless place." As he carried her luggage and guided her toward his car, he was trying to convince both Angel and himself.

When she calmed down enough to speak, Karlene told Oliver that her uncle lived on the other side of White Plains and they could try his place. But when Oliver drove across the city and saw the slum that was her uncle's neighborhood, he was appalled.

"This street is a home for b-bums and d-drug dealers," he told her. "I don't like it here, Angel." They were walking into her uncle's building. "It's n-not safe."

They started climbing the steps toward his apartment when suddenly Oliver stopped short and pulled her back. "I can't do it, Angel," he said with a new authority. "I'm not leaving you in this neighborhood. Let's go. We'll figure something else out."

She followed him submissively back to the car and as they pulled away they both noticed the heads turning to stare at what many neighbors thought was a cop car that they hoped was not there to make a bust.

In silence Oliver and Karlene rode out of White Plains. It was after midnight and Oliver, exhausted from the day, automatically drove back toward Long Island and to his house in Great Neck.

He knew that at this hour his parents would be fast asleep with their bedroom door closed. Leaving Karlene's belongings in his car, they tiptoed upstairs in single file, to his bedroom.

Minutes later as they lay naked together under his flowered bedspread, Oliver was trying to figure out a plan for finding a home for his Angel. As he finally fell asleep, he made a decision: Angel would live with him.

The next morning he waited until his father had left for work and then went downstairs to the kitchen, where he knew he'd find his mother drinking coffee and watching her morning TV shows. He hated to be late for work himself, but this was his only chance.

"Oliver, what are you doing here?" his mother asked, surprised to see him still at home.

"Mom, I've g-got a p-problem." To make her more comfortable he answered her in Yugoslavian as he sat down next to her at the kitchen table.

Her face immediately clouded with concern. "What is it, Olly?"

"Do you remember the girl Karlene who was here at the house one time?" He knew his father had told her about their confrontation at the front door. But he didn't wait for a response. "Well, she got k-kicked out of her home and she has no p-place to live."

Hoping to gain his mother's sympathy, Oliver told her, with few details, what had happened the night before.

"So I thought, Mom, that maybe she c-could stay here. Just for a little while, until she can f-find an apartment or something."

"But Oliver, your father—" she started to protest.

"He doesn't have to know, Mom." He put his hand over hers. "It's just for a short time. She can stay up-stairs with m-me, and he'll never know she's there. She won't b-be in the way at all."

His mother stood up abruptly and began to pace.

"Oh, Oliver, I don't know what to say. Your father would be furious. He'd never understand. You know how he is." She looked back at him, still sitting in the same spot.

Watching his mother pace, Oliver was picturing Karlene's face when her own mother had told her she couldn't come home. Other images flashed through his mind: of her uncle's neighborhood, of her packed bags waiting at the front of her foster home, and of Angel now waiting upstairs for him.

"Mom, I love her. You've got to help us," he begged.

She saw the look on her son's face and answered softly, "One week, Oliver. She can stay for one week, and by then she'd better find someplace else to live."

Oliver informed Angel that she had a new home—at least temporarily. Quickly he formed a plan.

Angel could leave with him early every morning and he'd drive her to school in New Rochelle on his way to work. Then he'd pick her up at the public library on his way home.

But Angel told him that she was having trouble in school; her grades had been failing and she didn't want to continue.

Oliver listened to her, unsure of how to respond. As he looked at her, he was overcome with the need to protect her and take care of her. Now that she would be living with him, she had nothing to worry about.

Remembering his own laziness and how much he had hated school, Oliver decided that maybe Angel was right. He agreed that she could drop out of school and he changed his original plan. After he left for work in the mornings she'd have to stay upstairs in his room until she was certain that his father was gone. Then she could move freely around the house but she'd have to leave by five o'clock because his father returned home promptly at five-thirty. When Oliver got out of work he'd meet her either at the Great Neck Library, at a local park, or along Main Street in Flushing, Queens, and they'd stay out until after his father's bedtime. And if, at any time, they heard his father coming upstairs, Karlene would run into the closet and hide in the back, behind Oliver's clothes, until the coast was clear. The arrangement seemed simple; whistling, Oliver left, an hour late, for work.

For the first few days Karlene rarely left Oliver's room. Once she heard his father leave she made the bed and cleaned his room, and spent most of her time watching his little TV, which she kept on a low volume. When she was hungry she nibbled on crackers that they kept in the room.

Finally, on Oliver's insistence, she ventured downstairs for a cup of coffee. On the first morning Karlene walked into the Petrovich kitchen, she met Oliver's mother.

"Good morning." Karlene greeted her shyly.

Startled, Anna Petrovich jumped, but quickly regained her composure. "Good morning," she answered in English with a heavy accent. "Would you like coffee? A muffin?"

"Yes, thank you very much." Tentatively Karlene sat down at the kitchen table while Oliver's mother busied herself preparing breakfast.

For the next hour they sat together and finished a pot of coffee while Anna asked Karlene about herself. She answered the questions honestly but cautiously.

After that, their morning coffee together became a routine. Karlene told Oliver about their conversations

and he believed that Angel and his mother were beginning to really like each other.

At the end of the first week neither Oliver nor his
mother mentioned their agreement, and Karlene
stayed.

Every morning before he left for work Oliver placed
a ten- or twenty-dollar bill on top of his stereo for
Karlene to have later in the day when she left the
house. He called home at his noon break to check up
on her and find out where she'd be meeting him that
day after work. When Oliver called, Karlene was often
helping his mother straighten up the house or sitting
with her in the kitchen watching TV. One day she
sounded especially excited because Anna had just
given her two bottles of Le Jardin perfume that she
said she never used. Another time Oliver heard them
giggling together and Karlene explained that they
were watching a comedy show on television.

"Don't worry, Oliver," his mother reassured him
over the phone one afternoon. "Karlene's a nice girl,
and everything is fine."

Oliver was beginning to feel as if the three of them
were a new family. When he pictured Angel and his
mother together at home, he smiled to himself.

Karlene told Oliver that she loved playing house.
With his money, she bought several small plants and
fixed up the guest room next to Oliver's bedroom to
look like a cozy den. They liked to pretend that they
were a married couple and that the upstairs was their
own little apartment.

Carefully, Karlene watched the clock during the
day. She was always sure to leave the house by five
o'clock. As arranged with Oliver during their noon
phone call, she walked to the library or the park, or

took a bus to Yonkers to the Pepsi plant where she waited for him to get off from work.

Knowing that they couldn't return home for several hours until Oliver's father was tucked away in his room and they could sneak upstairs, they often went to the movies. Inside the dark theater they sat close together, hands clasped, bodies touching, both willing the time to pass so they could return to Oliver's bedroom.

On one evening when they got home too early and Oliver's parents were still watching TV in the kitchen, Oliver suggested that they go for a drive around Great Neck. They stopped at a small park and, lured by the beautiful late spring evening, lay down on the grass under the intricate network of stars. Neither realized that they had fallen asleep until they were jolted awake by the lights of a local police car beaming down on their faces, and they had to explain to a police officer what they were doing in a park that had closed hours ago, lying on the grass, wrapped in each other's arms.

Back at the house they were always careful to keep their voices low and to move quietly. They found pleasure in just watching each other, having sock fights and stifling their giggles in Oliver's pillow, and lying silently together in bed—Oliver reading a mechanics magazine while Karlene played with the hairs on his chest.

But one day Oliver's father met a neighbor outside who innocently asked him what a black girl was doing in the Petrovich house.

Svetozar Petrovich excused himself as quickly as possible, stormed into his house and charged up the stairs toward Oliver's bedroom.

He grabbed the knob of the locked door and shook it violently.

"Oliver!" he shouted, banging on the door. "Open this door right now!"

They had heard his approaching heavy footsteps. "Into the closet!" Oliver had whispered to Karlene.

As his father pounded on the door Oliver was stalling while Angel pushed the clothes in his closet aside and crawled behind them. In only a few seconds she was well hidden and Oliver noiselessly closed the closet and went to open the door to his room.

"What is it?" He tried to sound annoyed to cover the fear in his voice.

"Who's in here with you?" his father shouted. "You never kept this door locked before."

"I d-don't know what y-you're talking about." Oliver was trying to pretend that he had been reading his car magazine.

"Why are you in here all of the time?" his father barked, as his eyes were darting around the room, from one corner to the next. "You used to spend all of your time outside with your car. Now suddenly you're in your room with the door locked." Anger was written on his face.

Oliver's father dropped to his knees and looked under the bed. "It's that nigger, Oliver, isn't it?" His tone had turned vicious. "She's sucking you dry, isn't she?" He tugged open the closet door, looked quickly inside and slammed it shut.

"Are you doing drugs, Oliver?" He was still shouting as he stalked over toward the bureau.

Oliver didn't move.

"That nigger is killing you, and you're so stupid you're like a blind man, and she's guiding you like a dog." Furiously he started opening the drawers of his son's dresser, picking things up and then throwing them back down. "Is she giving you drugs, Oliver? Is that it?"

Oliver just watched him but didn't say a word.

"That nigger bitch is no good, and you're so stupid you don't even see it. She'll rob you blind, and then it'll be too late."

Having come up dry in his search around Oliver's room, he started to leave, but turned back once more to look at his son. "You keep that nigger away from here—do you hear me?" And he slammed the door behind him.

As Svetozar Petrovich stormed back down the flight of stairs, Oliver sat frozen in place on his bed, and Karlene still crouched in the back corner of his closet, her head curled tightly into her body. Both were shaking.

Chapter 4: MAY 1977

"I DARE YOU, PETROVICH"

"There she is, Petrovich." Steven Harper pointed. "Ya got any guts, or are you all talk?"

Oliver looked across the school playground where Katy Lyons stood in the corner by the swings, talking to a girlfriend.

Seeing her with that smug expression on her twisted face reminded Oliver how much he hated her. He knew it wasn't her fault that a birth defect made her face look deformed. But on top of being ugly Katy was a goody-goody, the teacher's pet and a tattletale. Oliver hated her for being all of those things.

Since the school year started he had gotten in trouble at least a dozen times because of Katy Lyons.

From the first time she told their sixth-grade English teacher that he had laughed at her and made fun of her, and Oliver had to write a three-hundred-word composition on the meaning of friendship, he knew he should stay away from this girl. But he couldn't control himself. The more the teacher favored her, the more he hated her. The more she tattled, the more he picked on her. In one month he had been kept after school, given extra assignments, and sent to the principal—all because of Katy Lyons.

"I dare you, Petrovich." Steven's voice called him back to the present. "Come on, you love a dare." His classmate pointed to a pile of bricks leaning against the building. "Show that little cunt just how much you hate her."

Oliver looked at Steven's face, eagerly waiting for his response. He looked back across the playground at Katy Lyons, who was still engrossed in conversation with her friend as the two of them walked slowly toward the school. Recess was over and most of the students had already gone inside. Aside from Oliver and Steven, only a few girls were lingering on the playground.

Oliver had never been able to resist a dare. Something about doing what nobody else would do gave him an indescribable feeling of exhilaration.

As Katy came closer he stared at her, and as their eyes met for a fleeting second he was certain that a smirk crossed her disfigured face, and he was overcome by a sudden urge to hurt her. As if in a trance, he walked casually over to the pile of bricks, picked one off the top and, carrying it behind his back, headed toward Katy. When he was about eight feet from her he stopped.

"Katy!" He tried to get her attention.

As she turned around to see who had called, Oliver threw the brick at her head.

Minutes later Oliver was in the principal's office. Having just found out that the brick had barely grazed Katy's head and she had only needed several stitches where it had broken the skin, Oliver now had to explain to Mr. Dugan, the principal, that he had just been fooling around and hadn't really meant to hit her.

"Honestly, s-sir, it was just a joke. I didn't m-mean it."

"You didn't mean it?" he shouted as he slammed his fist down on his desk. "You threw a brick at this girl and you didn't mean it?"

Oliver looked down at his hands that were folded on his lap.

"You are so damn lucky that Katy wasn't hurt worse than she was," Mr. Dugan continued in a voice filled with contempt. "That poor girl has been through enough in her life, and she surely doesn't need a troublemaker like you to make things worse." He leaned over his desk toward Oliver. The veins on his bald head were bulging. "Do you understand me?" he shouted.

"Y-yes s-sir," Oliver answered softly, never looking up.

"I'm going to suspend you from school for three days, Oliver," Mr. Dugan said, a calmer authority returning to his voice. "You will make up all of your assignments, and you will write a letter of apology to Katy for this inexcusable behavior." He paused as if deciding what to do next. "Now I will call your parents to tell them what has happened."

As she had done many times before, Anna Petrovich covered for her twelve-year-old son and kept his suspension a secret from her husband. She had seen his anger directed against Oliver too often and feared for their son's safety.

"We'll tell your father that you're not feeling well," she decided as they left the school together, her voice and body trembling. "And for the next few days you'll be home with a stomach virus."

Later that night as he lay in bed thinking about the day, Oliver wondered if he would ever lose the empty feeling inside of him. For as far back as he could remember he had always been in trouble.

In first grade his parents had enrolled him in Catholic school, where they thought he would make nice friends from good families and get the best education possible. But Oliver had hated the strict nuns in charge of the school, who had made him sing songs whose words he could never remember and say prayers that he didn't understand. His only freedom had been at recess when he would escape to the playground, and for no reason he'd often run up to a classmate and punch him.

After two years of trying to philosophize with him, reform him, and save his soul, the sisters had thrown him out.

In third grade Oliver had started at P.S. 111 on West Fifty-third Street in Manhattan. As the new boy in school he had been the object of scrutiny. His classmates had stared at him because he was a head taller than anyone else in the class. They had giggled over his foreign accent and whispered about his stutter. Oliver became the one most often picked on by the other boys. When they left him out of their games during recess, Oliver stood alone in the corner of the playground or wandered aimlessly, and tried to pass the lunch hour by kicking pebbles between bushes that he pretended were goalposts. As he watched the boys playing and laughing together, intentionally ignoring him, he told himself over and over that one day he would get even.

The only one in his class who talked to him was a black girl named Vanessa. She told him jokes, shared her Life Savers with him, and offered to sit with him at lunch when she saw him alone in the cafeteria.

Even though she was a girl, Oliver was happy to have a friend. But one night during dinner when he told his parents about Vanessa and mentioned offhandedly that she was black, his father became enraged and beat Oliver with a broom.

After that Oliver spent more and more time alone. During school he rarely spoke to anyone, often daydreaming while pretending to be working on his assignments. Every afternoon as soon as he got home he took his bike and headed to Central Park, where he had memorized every path, and he rode around, often with no destination, until he knew that his father was on his way home from work and he had to race back to beat him to the apartment.

Oliver's grades fell and his third-grade teacher sent his parents concerned warning notes, which he intercepted and ripped up before they ever saw them. He knew that if his father saw his report cards he'd beat him.

Anna Petrovich, torn between loyalty to her husband and a maternal instinct to protect her son, hid the report cards.

As Oliver continued to withdraw further into himself, he found it easier to deceive his father, until the afternoon in fourth grade when Mr. Dugan called home and Svetozar Petrovich unexpectedly answered the phone.

There had been a fight in school, and Oliver had thrown a chair at another boy in his class.

By the time Oliver's father arrived at school, both boys were waiting in the principal's office. When Oliver saw his father instead of his mother as he had expected, he suddenly began to tremble.

In one motion, with his eyes only, Svetozar Petrovich assessed the scene. On two identical chairs at opposite ends of the office were his son Oliver and William Freeman, a black boy, almost as tall as Oliver. As he entered the office both turned from Mr. Dugan, who was sitting at his desk talking to the boys.

Oliver's father wasted no words. He looked right at his son. "What happened?" he demanded.

Oliver looked down at his lap. "He was p-p-picking on me," he answered softly. "He p-poked a s-stick at me and c-called me names. So f-finally I g-got m-mad and I p-p-picked up a chair and threw it. B-but it d-didn't hurt him."

His father looked hard at Oliver for several long seconds before speaking again.

"Get up," he ordered. He turned to the principal and addressed him in a voice filled with respect. "If it's okay with you, Mr. Dugan, I'd like to take Oliver home with me now. And I will deal with him appropriately." Not waiting for a response, he turned and marched from the office, with Oliver having no choice but to follow.

They were both silent as they walked to the front door of the school, Oliver with his head down, waiting for his father to yell at him. They were halfway down Fifty-third Street when his father finally spoke. "You okay?"

Taken by surprise, Oliver wasn't sure how to react. He nodded.

His father put his hands in his pockets and continued walking briskly, looking straight ahead. "That nigger deserved it. He was asking for it."

Oliver took the biggest steps possible to keep up with his father. His mind was racing, trying to think of what to say. But nothing would come.

Even before Oliver had understood the term, he knew that his parents were racists. He remembered an episode when he was six and a basement alarm had sounded in their apartment building. His father had run by him with a rifle and had intercepted two Puerto Ricans running out of the building with their arms full, dropping stolen goods as they ran. Hiding behind a wall, Oliver had watched as one fired a shot at his father but missed. His father aimed his rifle at the Puerto Rican's leg and fired. The second man followed up the stairs, crying, with his hands up. Oliver's father had kept him in the yard until the police came. The next morning on his way to school Oliver had seen a trail of blood on the sidewalk.

Over the years Oliver had heard the disgust in his father's voice when he told stories from the Canada Dry Bottling Company, where he was a supervisor, about the black workers who gambled away their weekly paychecks and then came begging for a loan.

Oliver remembered listening to his father tell one story about a black worker who threatened him with a knife, another about a nigger who had hit his station wagon and then taken off.

But Oliver's memories didn't make him any less nervous as he walked home from school next to his father. On the verge of panic, he heard his father's voice again. "I bet that nigger won't mess with you again." For the first time Svetozar Petrovich looked into his son's eyes. "We won't say anything about this to your mother. I'll tell her there was a little problem in school and we've resolved it. As far as the principal is concerned, I've dealt with you."

He turned away from Oliver and continued walking. "Now let's go home."

Oliver often didn't know what to expect from his father, who never again mentioned the fight with William Freeman or his visit to the school.

A few months later on the playground, when Oliver found a stray kitten which he named Pebbles after the ones he was kicking at the time, his father agreed to let the kitten stay in the apartment if Oliver took care of him. Oliver was amazed at how gentle his father was with Pebbles. He even brought home a ball of string for the kitten and let him cuddle on his lap while he watched TV.

But the pleasures of a family pet disintegrated the evening that Pebbles relieved himself on their dining room carpet. Oliver sat frozen in his chair and watched his father grab the kitten and start twisting its neck. His mother jumped up and tried to stop him, pleading, "Svetozar, it's only a kitten! Leave the baby alone!"

But his father wouldn't stop. Still holding Pebbles by his neck, he opened the apartment door and flung him across the hall where the kitten slammed into the wall.

Oliver, unable to watch, ran into his room. Later his mother assured him that Pebbles was not hurt, but she added that the kitten could no longer live with them in their apartment. Oliver never found out what his father did with the kitten and he never again saw Pebbles.

When his father made a decision, no matter how unfair it seemed Oliver never argued. When he hit him or punished him, Oliver never fought back. The only time Oliver ever felt free was outside when he was riding his bike. As he pedaled farther from the apartment toward Central Park, he felt his body begin to relax and thoughts of his father, his teachers, and his classmates began to fade. He could ride for hours, weaving in and out of the bike paths of the park. When he got bored Oliver headed to his other favorite place: a railroad tunnel on West Seventieth Street through which trains passed very infrequently. He had first discovered it when he was ten, and it had become his own private space.

Once inside the tunnel Oliver took long pieces of wood and constructed a series of ramps. Returning to his bike he practiced jumping, often pretending to be performing for a large audience.

In the tunnel, on the few times when Oliver heard the whistle of an approaching train, he quickly disassembled the ramps, pushed the pieces of wood and his bike against the side, and flattened his body up against the wall of the tunnel, waiting for the train to enter.

He often held his breath until the train had passed through.

After two years of jumping ramps and watching trains pass, Oliver sought more daring challenges. The week after he was suspended for throwing the brick at Katy Lyons, Oliver was riding his bike toward his hideaway when he heard the whistle of a subway train. On an impulse Oliver jumped off his bike and pushed it into the nearby bushes. As he sprinted toward the train tracks he saw the lights fast approaching. Oliver ran alongside the train, counting the cars as they passed him. When he spotted a car with a ladder on its side he ran closer to the train and, in one instant motion, grabbed the ladder and hurled himself up to the top of the car. On top of the train he felt elated. Oliver was jumping from one car to the next when suddenly he realized that the train was about to enter the tunnel. He crouched down, and just in time extended his body into a prone position. Lying on top of the train as it entered the tunnel, he barely fit inside.

As soon as the train passed through the tunnel Oliver sprang back to his feet, turned around and walked back along the tops of the cars. He felt like a tightrope walker, putting on a show for all of Manhattan.

But when one of the workers on the train spotted him on top of the car, Oliver knew that his game was over. Hearing shouts from an engineer who had stuck his head out the window, Oliver leaned forward and leaped from the train onto the tracks. As he jumped he felt something burn his left leg, but Oliver didn't stop to look. He felt as if he were in a movie, making his great escape. He kept running, back through the tunnel and toward the bushes where he had left his bike.

His leg stung, but he would deal with it later, he told himself, as long as he didn't get caught. If his parents saw the burn he knew he'd have to come up with a good story.

Oliver finally reached his bike and looked down at the blistering burn. As he rubbed his leg he was congratulating himself on the success of his daring adventure, and worrying about what his father would do to him if he found out.

"SEND HER BACK TO HARLEM WHERE SHE BELONGS!"

"Excuse me, can I help you?" A deep voice greeted Oliver and Karlene as they opened the front door of the Great Neck house.

Oliver's father had been looking out the front window when he saw his son's car pull up. He now stood at the entrance, in bare feet and dressed in boxer shorts and an undershirt, holding a shotgun and pointing it at the two of them.

Stunned, Oliver stood motionless and stared at his

father, while Karlene took a step back and tried to hide behind Oliver.

Svetozar's eyes were filled with hatred as he looked at them. Finally he lowered the gun and with contempt in his voice, spoke to Oliver in Yugoslavian.

"Get the fuck out of here!" he commanded.

Silently Oliver put his hand on Karlene's arm and guided her down the path, back toward his car. He drove once around the block, trying to calm himself down and decide what to do next.

A few doors from his house he stopped the car and told Karlene to get out, walk the rest of the way, and wait for him at the side of the house. Alone, in case his father was still looking out, he pulled the car into the driveway and waited there, watching the house.

When his father didn't reappear, Oliver ran to the garage, grabbed a ladder, and carried it to the side of the house where Karlene was waiting. Without speaking, he leaned the ladder against the wall and carefully helped her to climb up onto the roof. With his finger to his lips, he motioned for her to stay there until he came back. After a final check to make sure she was safe, Oliver returned the ladder to the garage and walked into the house through the front door.

He paid no attention to his father's heavy footsteps following close behind him up the flight of stairs, and closed his bedroom door.

Without knocking, his father flung it open and stalked into his room. "Oliver!" he bellowed.

Oliver sat down on his bed but didn't look up.

"Look at me when I talk to you!" his father commanded.

Oliver raised his head just enough to meet his father's eyes.

Svetozar Petrovich stood in the middle of the room, his arms folded, trying to control his rage. "That nigger is no good for you, Oliver. Can't you see that she's trying to use you and rob our house?" When he got no response he began to pace from one end of the room to the other. "Niggers are the top criminals in this country, Oliver, and this one's no different," he continued. "She's part of a gang and they all have a plan to rob us."

When his father saw that Oliver had again looked away from him he charged over to the bed and grabbed him roughly by the shoulders. "Listen to me!" he shouted. "You're a fool. That nigger is a fucking hooker. She's on drugs and she's going to soak you dry to pay for her habit. How blind can you be?" Abruptly he turned and walked toward Oliver's door. As he grabbed the knob he looked back at Oliver. "If I ever see that nigger in this house again, I'll kill you both."

Oliver couldn't move. He sat on his bed in the same position, with his hands clasped on his lap so tightly that his knuckles were white.

There was so much inside his head that he had wanted to tell his father. He had wanted to explain that the black girls he met didn't have the attitude problems so many Long Island white girls had. He had wanted his father to understand how much he loved Angel, that she was so much nicer and prettier than any of the other girls he knew. But Oliver never could talk back to his father and he hadn't been able to find any of the right words.

Oliver waited until he knew that his father had gone into his bedroom. Then he opened his window and motioned to Karlene, still on the roof, to come inside.

As she climbed into his room neither spoke. Slowly, silently, they undressed each other and made love on Oliver's rug. They clung to each other desperately, and when they had finished held each other tenderly and silently. Moments later, still entwined on the rug, they fell asleep.

Oliver longed to make his parents understand how good it was between Angel and himself, how perfect they were together. They found pleasure even in the simplest activities—like sitting on the bank of a pond in a small park in Great Neck, eating Dunkin' Donuts, watching the ducks and throwing doughnut crumbs to them in the water. When the ducks swam to shore and waddled fearlessly toward them, Karlene would shriek in fear and rush for comfort into Oliver's arms. Just holding her, kissing her, and protecting her made him feel a happiness he had never known before.

Behind the locked door of his room they would often argue playfully about who got to sleep with the flattest of Oliver's three pillows. But Oliver always let his Angel win, with the condition that she'd let him sleep the whole night snuggled up close behind her.

For Oliver and Karlene, weekends were the best part of the week because Oliver didn't have to rush out of bed early to get to work. On Saturdays he often woke up early, even without an alarm clock, and drove over to McDonald's or a nearby deli to pick up breakfast for the two of them, which he brought back, and together they ate breakfast in bed. They often stayed upstairs until noon, watching cartoons on TV, cuddling together, making love silently under the sheets.

After they heard Oliver's parents leave to do their

weekly grocery shopping and then check on the apartment building they owned in Flushing, Queens, Oliver and Karlene began to move more freely around the room. They showered, dressed, and usually left the house before Anna and Svetozar returned home.

Karlene wanted to learn how to drive, and Oliver loved to give her lessons. On some afternoons they drove up to Great Neck's most exclusive area, Kings Point, where Oliver let Karlene practice driving his car. Other times they went to Roosevelt Field, where they spent several hours browsing and shopping in a large indoor shopping mall, always hand in hand.

If Oliver's parents returned home before they had left the house, Oliver quickly helped Karlene inside the closet, making sure she was comfortable and well hidden behind his clothes, then he dutifully headed downstairs to help his parents bring in their groceries.

When Oliver and Karlene argued, it was usually over silly things that were quickly forgotten. She got angry with him when he spent too much time working on his car, she yelled at him for haphazardly throwing his dirty clothes around the room. But once Oliver grabbed her and kissed her, Karlene usually forgot about whatever had annoyed her moments before.

One morning while she was in the shower Oliver discovered that his *Playboy* and *Screw* magazines were missing from under his mattress. He was still looking for them when Angel came out of the bathroom, wrapped only in a towel.

"What's the matter?" she asked in a teasing voice that suggested she knew what he was looking for.

Oliver was still searching under his mattress. "Angel, where are my magazines? Did you see them?" he asked.

"You don't need them anymore," she answered him
smugly.

Oliver looked over at her and saw a pout forming on
her face. "You're jealous!" he teased, as he inched forward to hug her.

"Let go of me, you jerk." She tried to push him
away, but started laughing and lost her resistance as
she fell into his arms.

Oliver couldn't remember when he had ever felt so
content. The dream of becoming a real family was
brought even closer to reality in the middle of July,
when Karlene ecstatically informed him that she was
pregnant.

Oliver started planning how he could save enough
money from his paycheck by the fall to be able to
move out and get a place of their own. But from the
start of the pregnancy Karlene had severe cramps that
often left her doubled over and near hysteria. When
they didn't subside after a few weeks, they agreed that
it would be best for her to terminate the pregnancy.

As much as Oliver wanted their baby, he couldn't
bear to see his Angel in such pain. Without hesitation,
he took her to a local clinic and paid $275 for an abor-
tion. Oliver hurt for the loss of their unborn child but
was relieved to see that Angel's pains disappeared and
she seemed happy again. The night after her abortion
she couldn't stop kissing him, and for the first time it
was she who insisted that he sleep snuggled up to her
through the entire night.

He would do anything to make his Angel happy. But
as they continued to grow even closer, Oliver noticed
that the relationship between Karlene and his mother
was becoming increasingly tense.

For the first few months they had seemed to like

each other. Since his mother had agreed to keep their secret, she had gone out of her way for Karlene. She had even started coming upstairs to invite Karlene down for coffee or lunch. They had spent hours together while he was at work, and Oliver had such great hopes for the three of them. But he sensed that his mother's mood was changing.

His first warning came one night when Karlene told him about a conversation she'd had with his mother that morning.

"She asked me if I was adopted," Karlene reported to Oliver.

"Yeah? So what'd you say?" He was reading a car manual and only half listening to her.

"I said no, you jerk." She laughed nervously. "But Oliver, then she told me that you are retarded."

Oliver looked up suddenly from the magazine. His eyes were clouding with anger.

Karlene put her hand on his. "It's okay, baby," she reassured him. "I told her that just because you stutter doesn't mean that you're retarded." She was trying to act as if the conversation hadn't bothered her, but Oliver could see her lip quivering. She was having trouble looking at him as she spoke again. "Then she told me that I'm so pretty and I should find a better guy." Tears were beginning to stream down her cheeks.

When Oliver finished listening he was shaking. The next day he waited impatiently for the first opportunity to speak to his mother alone.

"Why did you say those things to Angel?" he demanded of his mother. "You know how m-much I love her and how m-much you hurt her."

Anna was straightening up the kitchen and stopped to look at Oliver. Suddenly she snorted and spit on the floor. "That girl is no good, Oliver. She's so skinny that she looks sickly." The disgust in her voice and on her face was obvious. "Besides, her hair is ugly and she looks like a bum in the mornings."

Oliver felt himself getting so angry he could feel the veins in his forehead throbbing. "You just wish you were as b-b-beautiful as she is," he answered back, hating his mother as he looked at her. "L-look at you, you're so fat and your hair is a mess. You're just j-j-jealous of Angel."

His mother spit again. "She's a slut, Oliver. And she's a nigger. There aren't any niggers in Great Neck." Her voice was rising. "She doesn't belong here."

Hearing these words from his mother, Oliver started to feel dizzy and held on to a chair to steady himself. "You're going crazy, Mom. You d-don't know what you're saying." He turned and bolted from the kitchen.

After the confrontation with his mother the tension in the house continued to mount. When Anna brought Oliver's clean laundry up to his room, Karlene found the few items of hers that had been in the hamper stained with black spots.

Oliver's mother stopped inviting Karlene down for breakfast, and once again she spent her time alone in Oliver's room.

Oliver thought things couldn't get much worse, when one morning Karlene woke up moaning in pain and told him that she had a problem with her liver and sometimes got painful infections. Oliver was frightened to see his Angel so sick but he had to leave for work. Counting on his mother's compassion, he hoped that when she saw Angel sick and in such pain, it would break her heart and bring his two women back together again. But when Oliver explained to his mother about Karlene's liver problem and begged her to take care of his Angel, she snorted at him with disgust and answered, "There's nothing wrong with her liver. That nigger has AIDS."

As the summer days grew hotter and more intolerable, Oliver realized that the living arrangement was not working out as he had hoped, and he'd have to start looking for an apartment for Karlene. His father would be taking a vacation from work at the end of September and would be home every day for those two weeks. He'd have to put more effort into saving his money, he decided, and find a decent place for Angel before then. Oliver sensed Karlene's growing frustration over having to sneak in and out of the house every day. Sometimes she had to wait for him at the side of the house or up on the roof for several hours, and he hated to see the pitiful look on her face, as if she felt like a beggar or a bum.

One evening, after having to stall for two hours until his parents finally went into their bedroom, Oliver went to the side of the house where he had left Karlene, to give her the signal that it was okay to come in. But when he reached the spot where he had left her, she wasn't there. Oliver was overcome with panic. Frantically he looked everywhere he thought she might have gone—the backyard, the roof, the garage—but he couldn't find Karlene. Not knowing where to go next, he started sprinting down the block, afraid to call out her name, searching down one dark street after another. His sides were cramped but Oliver kept running toward his final hope: the park where they often went to feed the ducks. When he spotted her, a lone shadow sitting hunched over at the edge of the pond, tears of both pity and relief sprang to his eyes.

"Angel!" he called, as he rushed over to her.

She was crying.

"Oliver, I can't do this anymore." She was choking on her words. "I love you, but I'm so tired of sneaking around like I'm some kind of tramp." She stopped to catch her breath. "It hurts so much."

"I know, Angel." He sat down next to her and gently put his arms around her. "It won't be too much longer. I promise."

Oliver felt as if he were on an emotional roller coaster. His moods swung from excitement over the thought of finding an apartment and moving out with his Angel, to the fear of facing his father and telling him that he was leaving. One minute he was feeling peaceful and content at the prospect of spending a Saturday with his Angel, when with no warning his father would call upstairs for Oliver to come with him to work at the Flushing apartment building. Karlene would then have to spend the afternoon in solitary silence, or sneak out after they left to catch a train to Brooklyn where one of her sisters lived.

Oliver hated the trapped feeling he got every time his father made him work in the apartment building. The chores usually took up the whole day and ruined his weekends, and Oliver was angry at having to give up so much time that he could have spent with Angel.

Many times as he walked through the basement Oliver thought about blowing up the building. It would be the only way he'd never have to work up on the roof or in the disgusting boiler room again.

Ever since 1974, when he was nine years old and his parents had bought the building, Oliver had been helping his father fix leaks and pipes, put in new sinks and toilets, paint and plaster. It hadn't been so bad when his mother came along on Saturdays. Sometimes they even went out to breakfast first and Oliver pretended that they were a happy American family. But more often it seemed that he got himself into some kind of trouble.

When his father sent him to do local errands on a bike that they left at the building, Oliver picked up whatever he had been sent for, and then rode up and down the streets of the neighborhood to kill time before returning to work. By the time he got back his father was usually furious with him for taking so long.

Oliver preferred working inside the different apartments, fixing leaks or changing sinks. He liked to snoop around people's homes and swipe something small. Over the years he had taken little toys, books, credit cards—always objects that were small enough to fit inside his pocket. Once when he took an Exxon credit card the tenant accused his father of stealing it, and that night Oliver was whipped and punished.

Another time, when he was fifteen, Oliver stole a small toy car from one of the apartments. The man who lived there must have been a collector, Oliver decided as he stuffed the miniature black hot rod into his jacket pocket. There were so many models of different cars, planes, and ships that Oliver never thought the tenant would notice one missing.

Later, when the man called his father, Oliver listened to their telephone conversation from the next room. He heard his father speaking in a very calm voice, apologizing for Oliver, making excuses for him that he was a car buff and must have gotten carried away when he saw so many model cars, and promising to locate the missing car and return it immediately. When he got off the phone, his father came to find him.

"Did you take a model car today?" he asked with great control.

Oliver didn't answer.

His father then picked up a stick, pushed Oliver to the floor with it, and started jabbing him in the stomach, again and again, while yelling obscenities at him for stealing the model. His mother, who had heard the commotion, ran into the room and stood frozen, crying out to her husband to stop, and helplessly watching the horrible scene before her.

As Oliver grew older the chores his father had him do became more time-consuming and demanding, and he grew to hate the apartment building more than ever. He overheard his father telling someone that the building was worth more than a million dollars, but Oliver wasn't interested in its value. All he really cared about was being with Angel, and working in the apartment kept him from being where he wanted to be.

When he thought about blowing up the entire building, he knew it wouldn't be very difficult. He could just loosen the few gas lines of several apartments' stoves, allowing the basement to fill with gas. When the gas reached the boiler room, Oliver was certain that the impact would destroy the building.

But as tempting as it was, Oliver knew he couldn't do it, because too many innocent lives would be lost.

No, he decided absolutely, he'd never do anything to hurt innocent people.

But he couldn't cope with his father's unpredictable behavior. Many times Svetozar Petrovich would be talking to Oliver in a calm voice and suddenly he'd become angry for no apparent reason and lash out at him.

Oliver had always been expected to put a portion of his paycheck in the bank, but in his need to save enough money for his future with Angel, he had started to withhold more money and hid it in an envelope in his dresser drawer. Not realizing that his father checked up on him, Oliver was shocked when Svetozar suddenly cornered him and demanded to know why he hadn't made a deposit that week. "It's that nigger hooker, isn't it?" he had yelled. "Why are you spending so much money on that damn nigger? Send her back to Harlem where she belongs!"

Later that day, when Oliver walked into the house alone, his father approached him and warned that he had just put acid on Oliver's shower floor. "I was trying to catch that nigger, just in case she was up there with you," he admitted. "If she dared to step into your shower she would have burned her feet and I'm sure she would have screamed." When his father laughed, Oliver thought he sounded wicked. "Then I would have caught her," his father continued, "and I could have killed her." He laughed again and stared at his son as if he were a stranger.

Oliver didn't know whether to believe his father. He ran right by him, upstairs to his bathroom, and without stepping inside the shower leaned in and turned on the water. As the water hit the shower floor a stream of smoke shot upward and a strong smell of acid permeated the entire bathroom.

The realization of what his father had done caused Oliver to burst into tears.

Later that night, when he told Karlene, he couldn't stop himself from crying. "And this was just because he thinks I'm going out with you!" he sobbed. "Could you imagine if he knew that you're living here?"

"Oliver, you've got to get a grip," Karlene told him firmly as she held him and tried to comfort him. "You've got to learn to stand up to your father."

But it was no longer just his father who was giving him trouble. His mother too put more pressure on him to get rid of Karlene.

"Oliver, find yourself a white girl," she had begun to nag every day. "Oliver, the nigger has to get out." And finally she reminded him of their initial deal, with a final threat. "Oliver, if she doesn't leave this house, I'm going to tell your father."

Chapter 6: APRIL 1979

"YOU MUST BE A BIG BOY NOW"

"Please don't tell my father!" Oliver begged his mother as she studied his report card. "He'll beat me, Mom. You know he will!"

Once again, as Anna Petrovich looked at the column of C's and D's she knew that she would have no choice but to hide Oliver's report card from her husband and hope he wouldn't remember that it was the end of the third marking period. She couldn't erase the memory of Oliver's first poor report card, in the middle of third grade.

Earlier that week she had bought Oliver a wooden plane for his eighth birthday. He lit up when he tore open the wrapping paper and played with the plane at every free moment. But when Oliver's father saw the report card—his first not filled with G's and E's but instead with U's for Unsatisfactory, N's for Needs Improvement, and teacher's comments that emphasized his need to try harder and improve his effort and behavior—Svetozar Petrovich's face turned crimson and he charged toward Oliver.

"This is unacceptable!" he had shouted as he slapped Oliver across the face. "No son of mine comes home with a report card like this!"

Before Oliver could react, his father had pushed him down on the floor and continued to kick him—on his arms, his back, and his legs.

"Stop! Svetozar, stop!" Anna screamed as she rushed to put herself between them and protect her son.

But Oliver's father had lost control. As if driven by an outside force, he started hitting Anna with the same fury. "You're just as guilty," he shouted as his hand slammed across her shoulder. "You bought him that damn plane!" When he turned back toward Oliver, Anna slipped away, and fell to her knees in the corner of the room.

Only when he had expended his energy did Svetozar notice his wife and son, both cowering in different positions in the living room. "You see?" he asked, as if expecting them to agree with his logic. "I've told you so many times that toys are bad for Oliver. They are responsible for his bad grades." He turned to leave the room, but looked back to add, "And we'll have to do something about this."

Later that night Oliver's father barged into his room with a large garbage bag and started rummaging through his drawers, sweeping all of his comics, baseball cards, models, games and other toys into the bag. The venom on his face made Oliver shiver as he watched his father tear the room apart and steal from him the remnants of his childhood.

Since that evening Oliver had kept any new toys he received a secret from his father. Whenever his mother gave him spending money he used it for a new collection of Sergeant Rock comics, which he carefully hid in the back of his closet. With birthday money from his grandfather he bought models of cars, planes, and Sherman World War II tanks—all of which he hid so that his father couldn't find them.

But Svetozar Petrovich never let up on Oliver. He continually scolded his son for any behavior that he considered childish. When Anna's father came to visit, Oliver loved to sit on his lap and listen to his hour-long stories of Yugoslavia. At the end of the stories the old man usually slid a few dollars, for good luck, into Oliver's pocket, with a little extra at his birthday and Christmas. But Oliver squirmed when he saw the look of disapproval on his father's face. Svetozar denounced his father-in-law for giving Oliver money and embarrassed Oliver for sitting on his grandfather's lap.

"You're too old to be acting like such a baby," he scolded him with disgust. "You must be a big boy now."

Every time his father found a model car or a comic that Oliver had forgotten to hide he became enraged. "You're too old to play with toys!" he shouted at Oliver, often hitting him. "And what's worse, you tried to sneak these things behind my back!"

Oliver tried to behave like a big boy and to hold back his tears, but he couldn't understand why his father was reacting so severely to the few simple things that meant so much to him.

Over the next few years, with gift money from his mother, grandfather, aunt, and uncle, he continued to replace his models, comics, and baseball cards. In eighth grade Oliver bought a model of a 1969 Dodge Charger and a set of enamel paints. Behind the closed doors of his bedroom while his father was at work, he meticulously assembled the model. He painted the Charger yellow with black stripes and added full details, inside and out, copying one that he had seen in a movie. For days after school Oliver spent hours in the kitchen carefully heating a knife over the stove so that he could create slotted-looking wheels by melting and carving parts of the model. When he was satisfied with the finished product he put it aside and dragged up a long piece of wood he had found in the apartment house basement, cut it with his father's saw, and painted it black to look like a road, with white lines for lane dividers.

Oliver had never been so proud of anything that he built by himself. Once all the parts were dry, he set up the display on his floor and pretended that the car was full-size and out on the highway. For hours his imagination took over as he acted out one scene after another.

But that night his father came into his bedroom before Oliver had a chance to hide it. When Svetozar Petrovich saw the model in the middle of the room he froze, but only for a second. With a burst of fury, he lunged at the car and gave it one violent kick, which sent it flying against Oliver's dresser. On impact small pieces detached from the car and flew across the room. Oliver watched in disbelief.

Oliver's father bent down and yanked the piece of wood off the floor. "Where did you get this?" he shouted. He held Oliver's highway over his head as if he were about to toss it out the window.

"F-from the b-basement," Oliver whispered.

"You stole this from the basement without permission?" his voice boomed.

Oliver didn't answer.

His father moved toward him with the wood. "You will take paint remover and clean this wood until not one drop of paint is left on it," he commanded. "I will check it to make sure it is satisfactory. Then you will return the clean piece of wood to the same spot where you found it."

He threw the wood on the floor. "Do you understand?" He was still shouting.

"Y-yes, s-s-sir."

Abruptly Oliver's father turned and left the room, slamming the door behind him. As Oliver started to retrieve the pieces of his car, his hands were trembling. He took a rag, dipped it in paint remover and methodically began to wipe the paint off the wood. While he worked he stared absently at the wood and wondered why his father was making him do this. He had seen so much wood in the basement that he knew no one could need this piece. His hands worked faster as he tried to direct his anger into the work ahead of him.

Oliver withdrew further from his father and tried to avoid him as much as possible. The less contact they had, the less he got into trouble. With his mother's help it was easy to keep secrets from his father: his deteriorating marks, the workshop that he set up in the corner of the basement, and his one friend William, his companion in model building, who was black.

Fascinated by the TV show "Starsky & Hutch," Oliver and William spent hours in the basement making copies of the .45 automatic guns their heroes used on television. They kept their supplies hidden in an alcove that only the two of them knew about. On weekends, with their handmade gun copies hidden under their shirts, they wandered into the lobbies of several of the most exclusive Manhattan hotels on Fifty-ninth Street along Central Park. When no one was looking they dashed into an unoccupied elevator and got off at any random floor. There they waited until they spotted someone walking down the hall, and in unison Oliver and William jumped in front of the hotel guest, pointed their guns, and shouted, "Freeze!"

Oliver got a thrill from the looks of terror on the faces of the guests who thought they were victims of a holdup. His ability to evoke such intense reactions gave him an invigorating feeling of power.

Neither of the boys was interested in anything more. Once they saw that they had succeeded in frightening their hostages, they staged a debate between them as to what they should do next, with one of them pretending to lose interest in the holdup.

It was usually Oliver who said first, "This jerk doesn't look classy enough for us anyway. He probably doesn't even have enough cash to make it worth our while." Turning to William, he directed the scene. "Let's let him go—what do you say?"

And on cue William would respond, "If you say so." Then he'd turn to the guest and add, "But you'd better keep your mouth shut about this. If you breathe a word about it to the hotel manager, you're dead meat. And we'll be back to find you."

While the two of them laughed and slapped each other five as their freed prisoner scurried away humbly and gratefully, Oliver was usually thinking about his father. He tried to picture his father watching the scene: Oliver and a black friend with phony guns, faking a holdup at the Plaza Hotel.

He shuddered at the thought of what his father would do to him. But it wouldn't happen, he reassured himself as he shook his head emphatically to erase the image from his mind. He was convinced that he had gotten too smart for his father, and from now on, no matter what he did he'd never let himself get caught.

Chapter 7:
SEPTEMBER 24, 1988
"FOR MY ANGEL"

Oliver wished that his parents would just leave him alone. But instead they became more aggressive in their attacks on Karlene and their insistence that Oliver meet a white girl.

"Oliver, if you could just find a nice white girl, you'd forget all about that nigger," his mother repeated to him every day.

During a brief moment together one morning before he left for work she started once again. "Oliver, remember Jack and Betty Walsh who lived near us in Manhattan?" She was trying to get his attention. "Well, they have a daughter Katy who's nineteen, and

I haven't seen her for a few years but she was always such a lovely girl. Sweet, polite . . . and white."

"Oh yeah?" Oliver wanted only to get out of the kitchen without an argument. But his mother persevered.

"I was talking to Betty Walsh a few days ago, and I invited their family out to Great Neck to visit. With Katy, of course." She hesitated, then finished her thought. "They're coming here to spend the afternoon tomorrow."

"What?" She had finally succeeded in getting his attention. "Mom, tomorrow's Saturday. I'm busy."

As if she hadn't heard him, his mother rambled on. "It will be so nice to have company. We can all have lunch out on the porch."

Oliver's father had also invited Phil Malone, the superintendent of their Flushing building, with his wife Dorothy, to join them for the afternoon, and had left instructions for Oliver to go to the store in the morning to pick up bread and soda that they needed for lunch.

Oliver was annoyed at the intrusion on his day with Angel and even angrier that his parents wouldn't give up trying to fix him up with other girls. But he knew better than to argue with his father. As usual Oliver responded with silent acceptance.

As he headed upstairs he was thinking about the last Saturday morning when he and Angel had had the house to themselves. It was one of the rare times that his parents hadn't roused him to come to work with them at the Flushing apartment, but left him to sleep.

He had awakened before Karlene and had quietly left the bedroom and gone downstairs for juice. While he drank he watched his mother's parakeets swinging on a bar in their cage.

Oliver couldn't understand why she made such a big deal over her dumb birds. Every time he looked at her favorite parakeet, Punkishko, he felt renewed anger that his mother could keep birds in the house while he was not permitted to have a dog or a cat.

But Oliver had given up all hope that his father would ever understand his longing for a pet, and he no longer even thought about trying to persuade him to change his mind.

With the luxury of time to himself, Oliver decided to indulge with a relaxing hot bath.

On an impulse he opened the birds' cage and took out Punkishko, leaving Mechkaro, the other parakeet, inside. With the bird perched obediently on his finger, he walked upstairs and into the bathroom to run the water in the tub.

Moments later he lowered himself, one inch at a time, into the tub, and transferred the parakeet onto his knee which was still raised above the water level. Only the bird's tiny claws touched the hot bath water.

"Come, you stupid bird," he said to the parakeet as he slowly submerged his knee into the tub and more of the bird's body went underwater with him. "How much can you stand, you dumb parakeet?"

Punkishko didn't flinch but just stared, with his beady little eyes, right at Oliver.

After a while Oliver grew tired of their game. He got out of the bath with the bird and walked over to the sink where he kept his hairdryer.

"We don't want to get in trouble, do we?" Oliver spoke softly to the parakeet as he pointed the blow dryer at the bird and flicked the switch to turn it on.

He was surprised that Punkishko continued to sit contentedly on the ledge of the sink while Oliver dried and fluffed his feathers. Only when he had finished and opened the bathroom door did the bird fly out of the room and back downstairs to the kitchen.

By the time Oliver came down to make breakfast, Punkishko had returned to his cage and was sitting peacefully on his swinging bar, staring at Mechkaro.

But Oliver was not finished. "Are you hot from the bath, dumb bird?" he asked as he again took him out of the cage. "Come. Let's see what we can do about that." Oliver opened the door to the freezer, took out a frozen muffin, put the parakeet inside the freezer on the same shelf with the remaining muffins, and shut the door. Then he proceeded to defrost his muffin in the microwave oven.

After the timer beeped he removed the muffin from the oven and removed Punkishko from the freezer.

The little bird was shivering. "Oh, don't worry, Punkishko," Oliver said in a soothing tone. "I'll fix that. I can defrost you too, in just a few seconds." And he put the bird into the microwave from where he had just taken the muffin.

By the time his parents returned home, Punkishko was back safely in his cage with no sign that he had ever left, and Oliver was relieved that their adventure would remain a secret.

But later that week while Oliver and his mother were in the kitchen together and the birds were roaming freely in the room with them, Oliver accidentally squashed Punkishko with the kitchen door.

When she realized that the bird was dead, his

mother became hysterical. "Are you drunk?" she screamed at him. "Are you blind?"

Oliver was annoyed by his mother's overreaction to a silly little bird. But the more indifferent he acted, the louder she ranted and the more hysterical she grew. He was beginning to lose patience and was barely listening to her anymore.

Suddenly she recaptured his attention when she screamed at him in Yugoslavian, "You don't even care about my precious little bird, Oliver! I'll seek revenge for this!" She spit wildly at the floor. "Wait till I tell your father about your precious little Angel!"

With his mind returning to the present, and the company coming over, Oliver realized that Angel couldn't stay in the house all day unless she remained hidden in the closet, and stuffing her in the tiny space for so many hours would be intolerable for both of them. The only solution, he decided, would be for Angel to visit her sister in Brooklyn, where she'd be out of the way.

The next morning after he returned from the grocery store Oliver spirited Karlene out of the house. They went to a nearby White Castle for a quick breakfast, and then he drove her to the train station in Flushing, from where she took a subway to Brooklyn. On his way home he stopped at a local automotive store to look for a book on computer control ignitions. His car hadn't been running smoothly and Oliver suspected he'd have to spend his entire week's paycheck on repairs. He had been planning to buy Angel a new outfit and was annoyed that he'd have to use that money on his car.

The day was not starting out well, he thought to

himself as he popped six Tylenol tablets to try to ease his throbbing headache.

Oliver had no intention of joining his parents with their company. He couldn't understand why his mother was making such a big deal over this Walsh family. She had even replaced their blue rug in the entrance foyer with a green one that she saved for special occasions.

To kill time while Angel was gone, Oliver decided to work on his car in the driveway. The clear late September day was comfortably mild and perfect for being outdoors, and he figured it would take him most of the day to take apart and reassemble his engine. By that time his parents' company would be gone and Angel could come home, he consoled himself.

When Phil and Dorothy Malone arrived at about noon, the four adults went around to the back screened-in porch to have lunch, leaving Oliver to work on his own.

Oliver spent the next few hours under the hood of his car, trying to concentrate on disassembling his engine. Three times he drove his father's station wagon to a local auto parts store, where he picked up several items for his car. At each visit to the store he used the pay phone to call Karlene at her sister's and make sure that she was okay. All through the afternoon Oliver's hands kept busy on the engine, but his mind was distracted by thoughts of his Angel.

Hardly fifteen minutes could pass without his checking the time, willing the minutes to pass more quickly.

The only good news for Oliver came at about two o'clock, when the Walshes called to say that they couldn't make it that afternoon because Betty's mother, who was visiting them, wasn't feeling well, and they didn't think it was a good idea to leave her for the afternoon.

When Anna told Oliver that the Walshes weren't coming, he wondered whether his mother was more disappointed because she had bought so much food for lunch, or because her plans to fix him up with their daughter had been thwarted.

While his parents were absorbed in conversation with the Malones on the back porch, Oliver sneaked inside to the phone and called Karlene again to tell her that the Walshes never showed up and that she should stay in Brooklyn until he called her again to tell her that it was time for her to return.

"You can't come back while Phil and his wife are still here," he whispered into the phone so his parents wouldn't hear. "So hang out there for a while with your sister and I'll call you when the coast is clear."

The afternoon dragged for Oliver. He was lonely without his Angel, and frustrated that he couldn't even accomplish the repairs on his car.

At seven o'clock that evening Phil and Dorothy Malone finally left. Shortly afterward Oliver called Karlene and instructed her to start heading home. Figuring that it should take her about two hours to reach Great Neck, he told her to hide in her usual spot at the side of the house and wait until he called to her from inside the front window that it was okay to come in.

As always, she agreed.

He had nothing to do while he waited. About an hour after he had called her, Oliver walked aimlessly into the kitchen, where both his parents were absorbed in separate activities. His mother was drying the dishes from lunch while his father sat at the table, engrossed in a situation comedy show on their small kitchen TV. Oliver sat down at the table next to his father and stared absently at the television, pretending to be watching, wondering where Angel was at that moment and wishing his father would get tired and decide to go to bed so he could freely watch for his Angel.

"It's a shame that the Walshes couldn't come today," his mother said in Yugoslavian to no one in particular as she methodically continued to dry and put away more dishes. "You know, maybe Oliver would have liked Katy, and then he'd forget about Karlene."

"Is that black bitch still around?" his father asked, his eyes still glued to the TV, his voice filled with hatred.

"Oh yes, she's still around. More than just around. Actually, Karlene has been living here, with Oliver, in his room."

Father and son both turned in disbelief to face her.

"It's wrong, Oliver," she continued, as if apologizing to her son for breaking their pact of silence. As the words tumbled out she wouldn't look at either of the men. "She's a nigger and she doesn't belong here. I'm sorry, Oliver; I couldn't keep the secret anymore."

Turning to her husband, her voice shaky, she finished what she had started out to do.

"It's only fair that you finally know. The nigger has been hiding in Oliver's closet for the last few months, and he's been sneaking her in and out of the house when you're not home or after you're asleep in our bedroom."

She turned to Oliver, as if pleading with him to understand. "I don't want trouble, Oliver, but I had to tell."

While his mother was speaking, his father's face continued to turn a deeper shade of crimson. He slammed one fist down on the kitchen table and shouted at Oliver, "Is this true?"

Oliver sat motionless.

"Is it?" his father yelled again.

Oliver hung his head and did not answer.

The momentary silence was broken by Anna's quivering voice. "It's wrong, Oliver," she repeated urgently. "She's a sick girl and you have to find a white girl. This—"

"Shut up!" Svetozar Petrovich shouted. "You mean to tell me that the black bitch has been living in my house? That nigger has been sleeping under my roof?"

He stood up and began stalking the kitchen, his voice getting louder with each new thought.

"That nigger bitch is poison! She's probably already robbed us!" he screamed. "I bet she has the keys to the house and she's told all her nigger friends about us and they're all laughing at us—planning to kill us and take everything we've got."

Anna, realizing that her husband could no longer be reasoned with, turned again to Oliver.

"It's better this way, Olly. She's no good for you. She's too skinny and she's sick. If only you can meet a nice white girl, who's like us, things will be better here."

She looked down at her trembling hands. Her recurring nightmare was unfolding before her eyes.

Oliver still did not move. Only the look in his eyes suggested the inner turmoil he was experiencing. Later he would admit that the battle between his heart and his mind started at that moment. His mother had turned on him. Now that his father knew about Angel, their life together was in jeopardy. He could bear almost anything, but not life without Angel. There was no way his parents could take his Angel away from him. He would do anything to keep her. Anything. Even if it meant getting rid of his parents.

"That nigger bitch is probably upstairs right now, laughing at us!" his father was still shouting. "I bet she's listening to us and laughing her black ass off. I'll go tell that bitch a thing or two."

He stormed out of the kitchen and up the stairs toward Oliver's bedroom. Still shaking, Anna was right behind him.

As his parents rushed from the room, the battle within Oliver was escalating. He loved his parents, but they were trying to take away his Angel. They were blocking his happiness. They said they loved him, but why couldn't they understand how he felt? Why couldn't they accept Angel?

Oliver's heart was pumping faster and more furiously. He felt as if on a dare he had just jumped off the World Trade Center, only to discover that he had no parachute. The panic within was starting to choke him, when suddenly he decided that with or without a parachute, there was no turning back.

As if in a trance, Oliver walked into his parents' bedroom. As he had expected, his father's loaded .12-gauge Remington automatic shotgun was behind the door. Oliver took the gun and, hearing his parents' voices back in the kitchen, carried it silently up to his bedroom.

Sitting on his bed, he examined the gun and methodically ejected three green shells from its chamber.

If there were more inside, Oliver didn't care. All he needed was three: one for his mother and two for his father. Three would take care of them both.

He carefully put the shells back in the chamber, stood up, and practiced aiming and flipping off the safety catch. Then, holding the gun tightly and still aiming it in front of him, Oliver walked slowly down the stairs.

He could hear his parents' muffled voices coming from the kitchen and he headed for the living room, where he carefully laid the gun under the couch, hidden from sight. Checking the time again, Oliver cursed to himself. The minutes were crawling by; it was still too early for Angel to be back. His palms were clammy and sweat trickled down his forehead.

Oliver's thoughts as he moved from one room to another were focused on Angel and how much he needed to talk to her, to touch her face, her hands, to see her smile. She was all that mattered, and he would do anything for her. Anything for his Angel.

Deciding that he had to get the gun closer to the kitchen, he took it out from under the couch and moved it to the dining room, sliding it under a chair next to the wall. As he listened to the voices of his parents and tried to hear what they were saying, Oliver paced silently from one end of the dining room to the other.

His mind was racing. He needed his Angel. He could never live without his Angel. No one could take her away from him. Anyone who tried would have to be stopped. There was no longer any choice. He would have to kill his parents.

Oliver looked out the window to see if Angel was there yet, but she still hadn't returned.

His mind was spinning. Should he kill them while they were together in the kitchen? No, he decided. He'd wait. First he had to see his Angel and make sure that she was home safe.

He knew that being next to her would calm his racing heart, settle the furious battle still going on within him. While Oliver continued to watch the clock and wait for Karlene, he heard his father leave the kitchen and walk across the hall into his bedroom to get undressed for bed.

Oliver couldn't stay still. His eyes darted furiously from the dining room window where he watched for Karlene to the spot under the chair where he had left the gun.

At about 10:30 Oliver finally spotted a dark shadow waiting patiently in the bushes at the side of the house, just as he had instructed his Angel to do.

Carefully he opened the window and called softly for her to come around to the front of the house. Gently, silently, he lifted her through a hallway window, and as they had done many times before, they tiptoed upstairs to Oliver's bedroom.

Safely inside with the door closed, sitting side by side on his bed, Oliver broke the silence. In a voice never louder than a whisper he told Karlene what had happened with his parents earlier that evening.

He started to cry. "Angel, you can't stay here anymore. What am I going to do?"

He shut his eyes tightly and frightening images filled his mind: of Karlene sleeping on the streets and begging like a dog for food. "I can't see you sleeping on the streets!" he cried.

"It's okay, Oliver," she said softly. "We can lock the closet and I'll sleep in there."

He hung his head and wept.

"Don't worry about it," she tried to console him. "It will be okay." She was wiping away his tears.

Suddenly his head shot up and he looked into her frightened eyes. Squeezing her hand, he said with a renewed strength, "It's over, Angel. I know what I have to do. I'm going to kill them."

"No, Oliver," she urged softly. "There are other ways. I can go live with my uncle in White Plains until we work everything out. It'll be okay."

"No, Angel." His voice was firm. "I won't let you leave me. We have to be together."

"Then we can both move out and get an apartment together," she persisted.

Still holding her hand, he hung his head. "It's no good, Angel. We have no money. How could we afford it?" Slowly he shook his head in defeat. "I've got to do it."

"But what would we tell the police?" she demanded, her panic growing. "It wouldn't work, Oliver. Please, Oliver, listen to me."

He stood up abruptly and pulled her up with him, regaining control of himself.

"Angel, I want you to get into the closet and stay there. Hide in the back, behind my clothes, just in case my father comes looking for you." He took her hand once more to guide her toward the closet. "And no matter what you hear, Angel, don't come downstairs. Stay right here."

Oliver helped her get into the closet, and when he saw that she was tucked into the back and well hidden, he closed the closet door and walked slowly from his room and back down the stairs.

His mother had gone across the hall to use the bathroom. Seeing that the kitchen was empty, Oliver rushed once more into the dining room and with one eye on the closed bathroom door grabbed his father's gun, hurried into the kitchen, and hid it under the kitchen table. He then slid into a chair and waited for his mother to come out of the bathroom.

When Anna returned to the kitchen she sat down across from Oliver. Mother and son looked at each other uneasily.

Anna spoke first. "You look tired, Oliver. Why don't you go up to bed?"

"Yeah, Mom, soon," he answered.

"We'll have to invite the Walshes another day. I think you really might like Katy." She forced a smile. "It was a pleasant afternoon with Phil and Dorothy. I'm sorry you didn't spend more time with us."

"I had to work on my car, Mom." He stared down at his hands as he tried to rub off the grease that remained on them.

"What are your plans for tomorrow?"

"I don't know yet."

She persisted in making conversation. "Did you finish the work on your car?"

"No, Mom. Not yet."

"Maybe tomorrow you will." She straightened a kitchen chair. "So where's Karlene?"

Startled, Oliver looked up. Was this a trap? For the first time since sitting down together, he looked into his mother's eyes, but he couldn't tell. He leaned closer to her. At this moment, with the battle between his heart and his mind still simmering, she was his last hope.

"Mom, you've got to help us," Oliver begged. "You

can convince Dad to let Angel stay here. I love her, Mom."

Anna turned away from her son and started to get up from the table.

"She's no good for you, Oliver. Your father is right. Black girls are trouble."

Anna was no longer eager to continue the conversation with her son. She left the room to get a box of bird feed from the basement, so that she could feed Mechkaro. When she returned, Oliver tried one final time.

"Mom, don't you understand how much Angel means to me? I'd do anything for my Angel. How can you betray me, Mom? I'm your own son. Your only son."

Anna turned away and started to leave the room. At that instant Oliver's inner battle was finally and absolutely resolved.

He jumped up from his seat, grabbed his mother from behind, swung his right arm around her neck and tried to squeeze her throat.

Anna, stunned, responded instinctively and frantically fought back. She tried to push his arm away, but was no match for her son and they both fell to the floor.

As Oliver momentarily lost his grip on her throat, Anna began to scream, and with a look of terror in her eyes desperately tried to pick herself up from the floor.

But Oliver was faster than his mother. He reached under the table for the shotgun, and in a split second aimed it at the back of her head. While she was still struggling to get up, he fired.

She fell instantly face down on the kitchen floor. As

Oliver looked down at her, a pool of blood began to form around her head.

He knew he had no time to think about what he had just done.

"What's going on?" Svetozar Petrovich's booming voice could be heard from his bedroom. "What was that noise? Anna, where are you? Oliver, what happened?"

As Oliver walked from the kitchen through the dining room, he could see his father in the boxer shorts and undershirt that he always wore to sleep. Svetozar was rushing back into his bedroom and reaching behind the door for his gun.

Oliver realized he had to move quickly. As he advanced toward his parents' room he aimed the shotgun in front of him and, still at a distance, fired at his father, hitting him in the stomach.

His father fell to his knees, groping for the gun that he still didn't realize wasn't there.

In one swift motion Oliver entered the bedroom, moved closer to his father, and fired a second shot into the side of his head.

Chapter 8: MARCH 1980

"YOU'RE GOING TO BE JUST FINE"

Oliver rubbed his throbbing head as he looked around the hospital emergency room, trying to figure out where he was and how he got there.

"It's okay," the nurse told him in a soothing voice that made him even more nervous. "You were knocked unconscious, but you're going to be just fine."

The last thing Oliver remembered was that he was driving his father's 1972 Plymouth Fury station wagon and turning the corner of Fifty-first Street and Tenth Avenue when he went into a skid. As he had done many other times over the last year, after his father had gone to sleep he had swiped his keys and taken his car for a ride around Manhattan.

But it had rained earlier in the day and by evening the temperature had dropped sharply, coating the streets with a thin layer of ice. Oliver hadn't realized how slippery it was until he sped around the corner and felt his front wheels slide. There was nothing he could do but crash into a tractor truck parked on the street. As his head hit the steering wheel, Oliver lost consciousness.

The nurse told him that he had been brought to St. Clare's by ambulance with a slight concussion and a bloody nose, and as soon as a doctor came to check him to make sure he had no further injuries, he'd be released from the hospital.

Oliver had been driving around without any ID, and knew that the nurse never suspected he was only fifteen. He tried to sit up, to focus on the room. His mind was clearing when he suddenly realized that he had no idea what had happened to his father's car. It had to be well after midnight, and his parents might have gotten up to go to the bathroom and noticed that he was missing. His heart was racing as the panic inside him mounted.

Still holding his head, he was looking frantically around the room, trying to figure out what to do, when out of the corner of his eye he saw his parents rush into the emergency room.

They had been summoned by a teenager from the neighborhood who had witnessed the accident and had run to the Petrovich apartment to get them.

They were all very quiet while the doctor examined Oliver. He confirmed that nothing was broken, and advised them what symptoms to watch for over the next forty-eight hours.

In the taxi on the way home Oliver learned that his father's car had been totaled. But there was no yelling, no hitting, no punishment. When they arrived at the apartment Oliver was sent to bed, and within the Petrovich family there was never any further mention of the incident.

Oliver wondered if his father knew that this wasn't the first time he had snuck out with the car. Soon after his fourteenth birthday he had begun his nightly adventures. At first his father's car keys were easily accessible, on a tray near the front door. But then his father had started taking his keys into his bedroom, almost as if he knew.

Oliver had waited for the first evening his father forgot to take the keys from the tray. After his father went to bed he had stolen out of the apartment, driven to a hardware store, and had an extra set of keys made for himself.

After that it had been easy to escape. Sometimes he rode through Central Park and followed many of the same routes he had once taken on his bike. The wooden police barricades throughout the park became tempting targets; when Oliver saw some ahead he often sped up and smashed into them.

On other nights he picked up his cousin Terry, who lived just a few blocks away, and they drove around together for an hour or two. With few cars on the road, Oliver loved to drive up the West Side Highway and pick his speed up to 100 miles an hour while watching Terry cover her eyes or listening to her scream in terror.

"Oliver, you're crazy!" she yelled at him after every

close call, while she tried to calm her trembling body. But when her cousin Oliver called to invite her out for another ride, she was always eager to go.

To Oliver a car was a place to have fun—whether it was driving at over 100 miles an hour on the deserted parkways of Long Island after midnight, or playing practical jokes on other drivers during daylight hours.

Every Halloween, Oliver wore a rubber mask of a celebrity or a grotesque monster. He liked to pull alongside other drivers to watch for their reactions. One year he bought a Ronald Reagan mask and drove along Northern Boulevard in Great Neck, waiting for a suitable car to prank. When he spotted two attractive young girls in a red sports car he quickly pulled ahead of them, cutting off their car. Anticipating their response, Oliver slowed down and watched the car speed up next to him. He waited until they were even with his face, then turned toward them, his Ronald Reagan mask grinning at them. As Oliver sped away he laughed to himself over the startled and comical expressions on their faces.

While Oliver loved to clown around on the road, he became enraged if anyone else tried to take advantage of him. When another car cut him off, he would follow the car until he caught up, no matter how long it took, then sideswipe it or ram into it before speeding away —just to prove that no one could get the best of him.

With each new car Oliver bought he became more fanatic in its care and maintenance. He checked the oil and water every day, worked on the engine on weekends. He never stopped worrying that someone would hit his car, and before getting in it each time he circled it three times to check for dents. Oliver was the first to admit that his cars were his true loves and his obsession.

Once, soon after he had traded cars with an acquaintance whose machine he had admired, Oliver changed his mind and decided that he wanted his old car back. He tried to reason with the man, who wouldn't agree to trade back. That night Oliver sneaked into the man's garage where his car was stored, switched the license plates, and stole back his car.

The experience gave him an unexpected thrill, and became the first of more car thefts. Oliver had no interest in keeping the cars he took, but was enticed by the challenge of figuring out how to steal them without getting caught. After he drove them around for a while he usually ditched them or sold them for small change.

But his streak of good luck ended—not for car theft, but for assaulting another student in school. A juvenile delinquency petition was filed against him, and since he was a minor, Oliver was forced to appear in New York City Family Court, where an agreement was reached and he was ordered to see a psychologist for six months.

The therapist, a young and attractive woman, asked Oliver many questions about school, his grades, his parents, his family life, and his hobbies. Oliver answered most of them in one word.

The psychologist spoke softly and tried to get him to talk about anything troubling that was on his mind or any problems he was having at home. Oliver liked the woman and wanted her to like him. For a moment while he listened he was tempted to talk to her, to tell her about how lonely he was, how confused he often felt, how frustrated he felt that his parents didn't understand him, how frightened he was of his father.

He even thought about telling her about his father's first life in Yugoslavia before he came to America, about his first wife and his first son, Dragon, whom Oliver had met when they all went the one time to Yugoslavia. And about the letter Oliver's father had recently received informing him that Dragon had been killed in a truck accident on the job. Oliver's mother said that Dragon was killed because he was a wild driver, and she was afraid that the bad luck would follow Oliver. Oliver had laughed at his mother. But later that night he had spied on his father in his bedroom, and had watched his father sitting by himself on his bed, holding tightly to a photograph of Dragon and sobbing.

Oliver thought about telling the psychologist so many things.

But the moment passed, and Oliver decided to keep his thoughts to himself. Stronger than his urge to confide in the therapist was his need to protect his parents, to guard their family secrets, and make sure they didn't get in trouble.

After his first visit, Oliver never returned.

Chapter 9:
SEPTEMBER 24–25, 1988

"ANGEL, I JUST KILLED MY PARENTS!"

Oliver couldn't move. As if in a trance, he stared down at the body of his father. Frozen in place, he was still holding his father's shotgun when he heard Karlene's hysterical cries getting louder as she raced down the stairs.

The sudden noise set Oliver into motion. He wandered into the living room where he knelt down on the floor, dropped the gun next to him, hunched over and began sobbing.

It was in that position that Karlene found him. "Oliver!" She burst into the room. "What was that noise I heard? Was it gunshots, Oliver?"

Oliver looked up at her but didn't move from the floor. "Oh, Angel, what have I done?" he cried. "How could I have d-done something like this?"

She came toward him and knelt down beside him, grasping his shoulders firmly. "Oliver, where's your father?" Her voice was trembling.

Oliver reached out to grab her. "Don't g-go into their bedroom, Angel. My f-father is in there."

With no warning the smoke alarm in the kitchen started ringing. They both jumped up and ran toward the noise. Oliver grabbed a chair and pulled it directly under the alarm. He stood on the chair, opened the case, and unplugged the battery. The blaring sound stopped as abruptly as it had started.

As they entered the kitchen Karlene had spotted Anna's body sprawled face down across the floor. Her hand had flown to her mouth to stifle the screams that were rising to her throat. She held on to the wall to keep herself from falling.

Oliver had pushed the chair back into place and was pacing back and forth from one side of the kitchen to the other.

"I have to call the p-police, Angel," he said between sobs, more to himself than to her.

"No, Oliver!" she cried. "They'll take you away! You'll go to jail, and who will look after me?" She was cowering against the wall, her hand still over her mouth, her body shaking.

Oliver, continuing to pace, was still crying. He walked to the front door, opened it, looked outside, then closed it again and returned to the kitchen. He stared at his mother's body, then rushed out of the room and into his parents' bedroom to look at his father. In a state of obvious confusion Oliver continued to tread back and forth, from one body to the other.

Karlene tried to follow him. "Stop, Oliver," she urged, trying to regain her self-control and to help him do the same. "You've got to wipe your fingerprints off."

Like an obedient child, Oliver went over to the gun and started wiping off his fingerprints with his T-shirt. Abruptly he stopped, went into the bathroom, and returned with toilet tissue, which he used to wipe the rest of the gun.

"Oliver, we have to get rid of the gun." Trying to take charge, her voice was quivering.

But it was as if he hadn't heard her. Oliver was deeply engrossed in his own thoughts. "We'll call the cops, Angel, and we'll say that we were upstairs when it happened. That we heard a noise, and when we came downstairs to see what it was, we found them." Absently he continued rubbing the gun. "No, no, that's no good," he decided suddenly. "I'll tell the police I did it, and then I'll make sure I convince them that I'm crazy, so they'll send me to a mental hospital instead of to jail." He stood up and began to pace again. "Yeah, that's it. I'll burn the car. Or maybe I'll set the house on fire."

Again Oliver fell to the living room floor. "Oh God, Angel, what did I do? I killed my parents!" He looked at her, his eyes filled with horror. "Give me the gun so I can shoot myself!"

"Oliver," she answered him gently, "come on. You have to get a grip on yourself."

He stood up again, picked up the shotgun, and started walking slowly up the stairs and to his room. Silently Karlene followed right behind him. It was the first time the two of them had ever left the door to his room open.

Oliver looked down, and noticing a few blood spots on his socks, pulled them off and handed them to Karlene. She put them into her pocketbook.

Oliver found clean socks in his dresser and put them on with a pair of boots.

"We've got to get rid of the gun, Angel," he said urgently. He picked it up from the bed where he had dropped it, carried it to the bathroom, opened the window and dropped it outside, listening to it fall into the dirt below.

"Come on, Angel," he directed. "Let's get out of here." Still in the same baggy brown trousers and Batman T-shirt that he had worn all day, Oliver led Karlene down the stairs and together they exited the house through the front door, leaving the front door open and the light and TV on in the kitchen. As the screen door closed behind them, the body of Oliver's father was still lying in a fetal position behind his bedroom door, and his mother was lying on her face on the kitchen floor.

Oliver went directly to his father's station wagon and motioned for Karlene to follow. Before he closed the car door he got out again and crept around to the back of the house where he had thrown the gun. He picked it up from the ground, carried it back to the car, and hid it between pieces of cardboard in the back of his father's station wagon.

Oliver pulled out of the driveway and drove down the street. He continued to drive aimlessly in silence, up and down the streets of Great Neck. Noticing that the car was low on gas, Oliver pulled into a self-service gas station where he pumped several gallons of gas.

Neither Oliver nor Karlene wore a watch but they knew that it was after midnight. Except for an occasional late night driver, the suburban streets were quiet.

Without knowing where he was going, Oliver kept driving. Both his hands gripped the steering wheel and he stared straight ahead. The car was approaching the Throgs Neck Bridge when Oliver finally spoke.

"This is where I'm g-g-oing to g-get rid of the g-gun, Angel." About three quarters of the way across the bridge, he pulled over to the shoulder and stopped the car. He put on his emergency flashers and lifted the hood. Then he sat in the car quietly, watching the traffic pass by, waiting for a gap so that he could make his move.

After a few minutes when he saw a wide enough space, Oliver looked once again at Karlene, reached to the back of the station wagon for the gun and got out of the car. Slowly he walked around the rear of the car to the passenger side, leaned over the railing of the bridge, and dropped the gun over the side. He never heard a splash and wasn't sure whether the gun had landed in the water or somewhere on land.

Back inside the car Oliver continued driving over the Throgs Neck Bridge and paid the toll. Suddenly he turned to Karlene, who was still shaking and had not said a word.

"Angel, we n-need an alibi," he said. "We've g-got to g-go back into Manhattan."

At the first opportunity he turned the car around and drove back over the bridge and into Manhattan. "We'll go to the g-g-garage where Wally works," he said. "M-maybe he'll b-be there."

He headed to the taxi garage on Fifty-third Street between Tenth and Eleventh avenues and walked inside to look around for anyone he might know. But none of the few men in the garage looked familiar.

Oliver was feeling more frantic with each passing minute. He stopped in front of a McDonald's on Fifty-sixth Street, left the car on the street, and instructed Karlene to follow his lead.

They went inside and up to the counter where Oliver ordered cheeseburgers for both of them. Desperate for an alibi, he tried to draw attention to himself and Karlene by talking loudly and kissing her passionately in front of the cashier.

"That was good, Angel." Oliver spoke softly to Karlene when they were at a small table. "They'll remember us: a black girl and a white guy, making out on line."

Karlene reached across the table to hold his hand. "Oliver," she said, "you need someone to hold you."

His eyes opened wider. "Angel, I just killed my p-parents!" Then, as if a new thought entered his mind, he added, "I think I should take off from work Monday and Tuesday to go to their funeral." He continued rambling. "I have to take off M-Monday anyway to bring my car into Chrysler. I'll go back to work on Wednesday." He looked down at his cheeseburger and started crying. "Oh, Angel, we're g-going to be number-one suspects! I'll definitely be arrested!" He buried his head in his hands.

"No, Oliver, no!" Karlene cried.

When Oliver saw the panic on her face he tried to regain his own self-control. "Come on, we have to g-go b-back to the house, and p-p-pretend that we just c-came home and found them."

As they were leaving McDonald's, Karlene remembered Oliver's bloodstained socks in her pocketbook. She gave them to Oliver, and on the way out he dumped them in the garbage.

During the ride home to Great Neck, Oliver was careful to stay within the speed limit. When they pulled up to the house at 64 Richard Avenue they gave each other a final look of silent acknowledgment, that just in case anyone might be watching, they would go through with all the motions of their prearranged plan.

They walked up to the front door, which was still open as they had left it several hours earlier. Oliver opened the screen door and forced a look of concern on his face. He called into the house, "Mom? Is anyone home?"

Turning to Karlene he whispered, "Remember, Angel, the front door is open; the screen is closed but unlocked."

He returned to his car, backed it down the driveway so that it faced the house, and turned on the headlights to shine on the front door. Then he returned to the door and called in again. In a voice loud enough that anyone nearby could hear, Oliver said to Karlene,

"I don't like this. Let's go next door to John's and get help."

Together they ran across the grass and rang the front doorbell of John Lambert.

After a few minutes a bleary-eyed man in his early forties, obviously awakened from a sound sleep, opened the front door.

"Who is it?" he barked. "What's going on?" When he saw Oliver and Karlene standing there, his voice softened. "Oliver, what's wrong? What are you doing here in the middle of the night?"

"I'm s-sorry to b-bother you, John," Oliver answered tentatively, "but we just g-got home and something doesn't seem right at my house. The front d-door was open and when I called in the house, no one answered. I think there may be some kind of t-trouble."

John came outside on his front porch and looked toward the house next door. "Come on in," he said. "I'll call the police."

He disappeared inside. Oliver heard him make the phone call, and within a minute he was back carrying a flashlight in one hand and a rifle in the other. "Let's go," he directed. "While we wait for the cops, we'll check it out."

The three of them walked back to the Petrovich house, with John leading the way, Oliver and Karlene following timidly and holding hands. When they reached the front of the house John peeked into the front window. "Nothing," he muttered. "Let's look around back."

Fearlessly he continued his search, walking around the side of the house toward the back porch. When he reached the kitchen window he stopped and looked inside. Oliver, watching him intensely, saw the drastic change in his expression as he spotted the body on the floor. Oliver held his breath.

But John didn't give any indication that he had seen anything out of the ordinary. "Come on, kids," he said calmly. "Nothing's here. Let's go back to the street and wait for the cops, just in case there might be a burglar inside."

They didn't have to wait long. The first police cars arrived at 4:50 A.M. and within minutes the peacefulness of the early morning erupted into loud confusion.

The first uniformed officers went inside through the front door and returned immediately to call for backup. Oliver's head was spinning as police cars and ambulances continued to invade his driveway. He stood on the sidewalk with Karlene and John, watching the scene as if it were a movie. The sun hadn't yet risen and Oliver was shivering from the chill of the early morning air.

When the first officer emerged from the house, Oliver asked him, "Are my parents in the house?"

"Yes, they are," he answered. "They're both seriously injured, and we have an ambulance responding to the scene." He asked Oliver if he would please stay in the driveway, then turned to Karlene and asked her if she would like to go next door, where she would be warmer and more comfortable. He promised Oliver he'd take care of her.

Oliver started to walk toward Karlene but a woman police officer stopped him. "Please," she ordered. "Stay over there. Please."

Oliver's dream continued as he watched his Angel being whisked away from him.

Another officer asked him if he would mind getting

into a police car to answer some questions. He nodded his consent but inside, he felt so confused.

Lights were flashing; police radios were blaring. Oliver listened to voices that identified themselves as homicide detectives and supervisory police officers. He overheard several of them discussing the situation inside and its possibilities: double suicide, murder-suicide, or double murder.

As Oliver was gently ushered toward a police car, only one thing was on his mind: Why had he been separated from his Angel?

Chapter 10: JUNE 1984

"GOOD-BYE, LITTLE PUPPY"

The pitiful-looking puppy wandering around the junkyard must have been separated from his mother, Oliver thought as he bent down and scooped it up. Oliver cupped the shivering ball of fur in his hands.

"It's okay, little guy," he said gently. "Don't worry; you'll be all right."

Holding the puppy, he walked around the yard looking for its mother. "Poor baby," he consoled it. "Don't you worry. I'll take you home with me and give you a new family."

As he thought about bringing home a pet to celebrate their recent move to a house on Long Island, Oliver's excitement grew.

His father had been talking about moving out of New York City for years. After escaping from Yugoslavia and coming to America on a banana boat, the crime-infested section of Manhattan known as Hell's Kitchen was not what he wanted for his family. His dream of a nice house on a quiet street in the suburbs had finally come true for himself, his wife, and his son.

Oliver drove home with the puppy nuzzled next to him on the front seat.

"Welcome to your new home, puppy," Oliver said to his tiny pet when they reached his bedroom upstairs. "We'll keep this our secret until you're trained." He put newspaper down on the floor and out of an old shirt made a bed for the puppy. When the kitchen was empty he sneaked up a saucer of milk and gently helped his puppy drink it.

For several days Oliver kept the puppy a secret from his parents. But one morning when his mother took his clean laundry upstairs she heard a scratching noise coming from his room, and when she went to investigate she found Oliver's new pet.

"I'm sorry, Oliver," she told him later. "But you can't keep this dog. You know how your father feels about pets."

Oliver realized that he had no choice but to get rid of his puppy. He took it to a local playground where many of the neighborhood children came to play. It would be the perfect spot for his puppy to be found and adopted by a loving family.

"Good-bye, little puppy," he said sadly as he left him in the middle of the playground.

But even after Oliver got home the pitiful face of the little dog continued to haunt him. He got back into his car and drove back to the playground. For almost an hour he combed the grounds and surrounding areas, searching for the puppy, but he never found it. Oliver finally returned home, hoping that the baby had been found and rescued.

For as far back as he could remember, Oliver had longed for a pet—a dog or cat that could become part of the family. But his father had always insisted that pets, like toys, would be a bad influence on him. And after witnessing how his father had treated his kitten Pebbles, Oliver had never again asked for a pet.

While still living in Manhattan, Oliver often passed by Macy's on Thirty-fourth Street, and if he had any extra time he went inside and headed right for the pet department, where he watched the animals. Several times when no one was looking, Oliver took a handful of small goldfish out of their tank and dropped them into another tank nearby filled with larger fish. He stayed just long enough to watch the big fish begin their attack on the smaller ones, then he nonchalantly wandered away.

If the fish department was too crowded Oliver went instead to the bird section, where he walked down the aisles opening the cages to let the birds out to fly. By the time the birds were loose and the manager realized what had happened, Oliver was on his way out of the store.

After the Petrovich family moved to Great Neck, Oliver occasionally drove by a local animal shelter, a home for abandoned dogs and cats.

On one morning he noticed a dog wandering around outside. She was low to the ground with long, floppy ears, and when Oliver got closer he realized that she was pregnant. When he walked toward his car, the dog followed. On an impulse, Oliver picked up the dog, dropped her in the trunk of his car and drove off. But by the time he got home Oliver realized that he couldn't keep the dog, and he didn't know what to do with her.

With the dog still inside his trunk, Oliver drove over to his friend Danny's apartment house in Queens and told him of his dilemma. After discussing several possibilities the two of them drove to a desolate spot along Jamaica Bay. They took the dog out of the trunk and put her on the ground. As they walked toward the water, the dog waddled after them. They were standing on a mound of large rocks when Oliver suddenly reached down, picked her up, and threw her into the water. Next to him, Danny roared with laughter.

They both watched in surprise as the dog quickly surfaced and started swimming toward shore. As soon as she reached land, Oliver picked her up again and hurled her farther into the bay. But again, she swam right back to them.

Oliver hadn't planned on such difficulty in getting rid of the dog. He was angry that their plan wasn't working. The pregnant dog had reached the rocks and was panting from exhaustion. She stood next to Oliver, looking at him with big brown eyes that made him even more furious. Abruptly he took off his belt and started whipping the dog. He and Danny then used his belt to tie the dog to the bumper of his car, and drove at 40 miles an hour in circles several times around the empty parking lot.

When Oliver finally stopped and went around to the back to dispose of the dog's body, he was horrified to find that the dog was still alive.

Infuriated and further encouraged by Danny, Oliver

threw the pregnant dog into the trunk and drove to nearby train tracks, where the two of them tied her paw to the track, knowing that within minutes a passing train would put an end to her. While they waited they threw the largest rocks they could find at the dog's head. But after a few minutes Oliver realized that it wouldn't be necessary to wait for the train, because the dog was finally dead.

With no warning he burst into tears and became so hysterical that he couldn't breathe.

Later that night, as Oliver lay alone in his bed, he tried to figure out why he had done such cruel and horrible things to a helpless dog. But he had no answers. For the next month he had recurring nightmares about the dog, and the awful humanlike noises she had made while she was dying.

But there were also times when Oliver went out of his way to help animals in distress. Just a few weeks after the episode with the pregnant dog, he and Danny found a baby sea gull at Jones Beach. Oliver brought it home and tried to put it in the same cage with his mother's two parakeets. But when his father saw the extra bird, he demanded that Oliver get rid of it.

That night Oliver drove by himself the half hour back to Jones Beach and, carefully holding the bird in a small basket, wandered up and down the beach trying to decide what to do with it. He figured that if he held the basket over his head, high up in the air, the bird's parents would see it.

"Hey!" he called out into the air. "I'm returning your baby. Come get him!" If they didn't see him, maybe they heard him, Oliver hoped, as he gently placed the basket down in the sand.

He walked back to the parking lot, where he noticed

that another car had parked so close to his that he could barely open his door. Oliver suddenly felt anger rising inside of him. He opened the trunk of his car, pulled out a pocket knife he kept there, and in one fast move flattened two tires on the neighboring car.

While Oliver drove home, when he wasn't picturing the reaction of the driver upon discovering his slashed tires, he was wondering if the baby sea gull had found its parents.

Over the years some of Oliver's worst dreams were about incidents with animals. Since he was little and had traveled to Yugoslavia with his parents he had often dreamed about the gruesome scene he had witnessed there. Several men had held a pig by its four legs while his father cut out its stomach with a knife. The pig was screaming and his father kept cutting, stopping only when the pig's screams finally ceased.

Oliver's worst recurring nightmare stemmed from the hunting trips upstate he used to take with his father. He had always hated it when his father shot at harmless deer, and had begged him to go farther north to hunt wolves and bears instead, or even to Africa to hunt lions. Oliver had finally told his father that he didn't want to go with him anymore. But even after he stopped hunting, Oliver continued to dream about their trips, except that in his dreams he was the prey and his father was after him. The nightmares still continued in the morning when his father returned from his expeditions. There was always a deer strapped across the top of his station wagon, and Oliver was convinced that the dead eyes were staring right at him.

Chapter 11:
SEPTEMBER 25, 1988

"WOULD YOU MIND ANSWERING SOME QUESTIONS?"

Oliver got into the backseat of one of the police cars parked in his driveway. A uniformed officer reached in, opened the window, turned a light on inside the car, and then closed the door.

Sitting alone in the car, Oliver continued to watch the scene unfolding outside his house. A short fat policeman with a bushy black mustache started to tie yellow tape from a curbside tree to one on the lawn, to prevent anyone from walking on the property. While he worked he was talking to several other officers. Within minutes the number of police cars, ambulances, uniformed officers, and detectives in suits multiplied faster than Oliver could count.

Still dressed in a T-shirt and slacks, Oliver felt cold. He banged on the window to get the attention of a police officer. "Hey," he asked. "Could I close the window in this car?"

The policeman looked at him. "No, you can't," he answered curtly.

"Then could I g-get my car k-keys from that lady cop over there, and get my black leather jacket out of my car? It's in the back of the driveway."

The officer looked over toward the female officer Oliver was pointing to.

"She took my keys to move my f-father's station wagon from the sidewalk where I left it," Oliver explained.

Again, Oliver's request was denied. But the officer opened the trunk of the police car and pulled out several white bed sheets, which he gave to Oliver. Oliver immediately wrapped them around his shivering body.

He was both fascinated and frightened by the flurry of activity around him. New police officers kept arriving in marked and unmarked cars, showing their ID cards and entering his house. Oliver figured there must be about twenty marked police cars parked on both sides of the street. Several officers stood in the center of the street, directing the traffic of early morning rubberneckers. Small groups of other officers congregated on the sidewalk and in the driveway, talking to one another and then turning to stare at Oliver inside the car.

One of them, Detective Brian Parpan, the carrying detective on the case, had been awakened from a deep sleep just a short time before, and had arrived at 64 Richard Avenue at 6:10 A.M. A homicide detective for the past two years, he knew what was expected of him and walked routinely through the house.

He saw silverware on the dining room table and at first thought there could have been a burglary of some sort, but on closer inspection noticed that the silverware was neatly stacked.

Anna and Svetozar Petrovich had been pronounced dead by medical examiner Michael Wiley at 5:27 A.M. Both bodies still lay in a considerable amount of blood.

When Detective Parpan entered the kitchen he grimaced at the sight of Oliver's mother, whose mouth had been completely blown away and whose tongue had shot across the room and landed on the kitchen counter, where it still lay.

He noted with curiosity that Anna Petrovich, in her sprawled position on the floor, was not wearing any underwear.

The Crime Scene Search Unit spent the next four hours examining the house, taking fingerprints and photographs and picking up bullets. They found twenty-one lead buckshot pellets: eleven on the kitchen floor, five on the dining room floor, and five on the kitchen counter. While they were progressing methodically through the house Detective Parpan walked next door to the Lambert residence, where Karlene was still waiting with a female police officer. She was extremely restless.

"Could Oliver come inside and be with me?" she asked the woman officer.

"No, he has to stay there," she answered.

"How's Oliver?" she persisted. "Could I please go outside and see him?"

"I'm sorry. No." The police woman gently put her hand over Karlene's arm. But Karlene got up, walked out of the living room and to the front door, from where she saw three other officers on the doorstep.

"Please," she begged them, "can I see Oliver?"

"No," one of them answered. "You have to stay inside."

"Where's Oliver?" she pleaded.

"He's okay," the officer said gently. "Now you stay in the living room."

She had just returned to the living room when Detective Parpan arrived. He sat down on the couch with Karlene and asked her to tell him where she had been and what she had done over the last twenty-four hours.

Step by step she recounted the day's events, keeping to every detail of the story she had planned with Oliver.

Meanwhile Oliver was still sitting in the same police car, with several different detectives taking turns sitting with him in the car and asking him questions.

Detective Vincent Donnelly of the Nassau County Homicide Squad approached the car, reached inside, and hit the power button to open the back window so he could talk to Oliver from outside the car. After a few minutes he climbed into the backseat next to Oliver and identified himself. Then he asked, "Are you Oliver Petrovich?"

"Yes, I am," Oliver answered, not looking at him.

"How old are you?" Detective Donnelly asked.

"Twenty-three. I was born on January 8, 1965."

The detective looked hard into his eyes. "Oliver, you know it's a tragic situation here. But I'd like to know some of the things that happened here on Saturday."

"Okay," Oliver answered softly, still looking straight ahead. As if on cue, he began his rendition of the events of the last few hours. "I g-got up between eight and n-nine, and went to the store to b-buy bread, b-b-because there were people coming over. Then about eleven I started working on my c-car." He hesitated, as if trying to remember the rest of the events of the day. "At about noon Phil, the super of my father's building, and his wife c-came over and they stayed all afternoon, b-but I stayed in the d-driveway and worked on my c-car." Again he paused. "Then at abbout 10:30 at night I went to the store and then I p-picked up my g-girlfriend in Douglaston. Her name is K-Karlene F-Francis. Then we went into the city, and we g-got back to my house at about 4:30 this m-morning."

"Then what happened?" Donnelly led Oliver.

Oliver seemed to think again, then continued. "When I g-got home, the door was open. The screen door was closed but unlocked and I was afraid to go in. I called in, b-but there was no answer. I called in through the front window, but there was still no answer." He stopped to take a deep breath. "Then I walked down the d-driveway to the b-back of the house and I looked in the kitchen window. I couldn't see anything, b-but the lights were on. So I went next door to my neighbor John Lambert's house."

"Why?" Donnelly asked.

"I was afraid I could get killed."

At that point Detective Donnelly stopped his questioning, got out of the car, and went back into the house to report to Detective Parpan what he and Oliver had talked about. They were both bothered by Oliver's account of looking in the kitchen window and not seeing anything, because when they had looked through the window, Anna Petrovich's body was clearly visible.

Detective Donnelly returned to the police car where Oliver still sat, staring straight ahead.

"Oliver," he said, "based on all of the activity at the house, will you object to going back to the police precinct to continue an interview with some other officers?"

Without looking at him, Oliver answered, "Fine."

Before he walked away Detective Donnelly told Oliver, "Karlene will also be brought back to the precinct."

Oliver continued to wait. The minutes passed and no one else came to talk to him. Finally a uniformed officer told him to get out and directed him into an unmarked police car. One detective drove and another sat in the back next to him.

Seeing no handcuffs or restraints of any kind, Oliver felt himself begin to relax and to think that maybe he wasn't a suspect after all, and he wouldn't be arrested.

As the driver started down the street he asked Oliver, "Is anyone in your family a cop?"

"No," he answered.

"The reason I asked," the detective continued, "is that I saw an unmarked police car in the back of the driveway."

"That's m-my car." Oliver still looked ahead, making eye contact with no one.

"Do you like cops?" the driver asked him.

"Yeah." His voice had the first hint of enthusiasm.

"I'm even scheduled to take the New York City Police exam on October 20."

Both detectives wished Oliver good luck.

They arrived at Nassau County Police Headquarters at 7:40 A.M. and parked by the gas pumps in a big parking lot filled with police cars and vans. They were still sitting in the car when another unmarked police car pulled up next to them, and Detective Parpan and Karlene got out.

Outside of the two cars, Oliver and Karlene rushed toward each other and immediately reached for each other's hands. Together they were escorted into police headquarters and up to the homicide squad offices on the second floor.

Still holding hands, they were ushered inside, and after a moment, when they least expected it, they were separated.

Chapter 12: MAY 1985

"HAPPY MOTHER'S DAY"

It was always when he least expected it that his father got the angriest. Oliver had thought his father would be proud of him for his generous intentions. Next Sunday was Mother's Day, and now that he was working and had saved some money of his own, Oliver wanted to do something especially nice for his mother and take her out for dinner. There were many fine restaurants in Great Neck and he was anxious to see which would entice her.

But before she even had a chance to choose, his father had exploded and forbidden them to go out. Oliver didn't understand his explanation that his mother shouldn't go out because in the custom of Eu-

ropean families her place was to stay at home. All he
saw was the disappointment on her face that she
wouldn't be able to enjoy the special Mother's Day
dinner that her son had planned.

He could hardly remember his mother ever leaving
the house. She spent her days at home; she took great
pride in her vegetable garden and the flowers that surrounded the house, and almost daily she swept the
sidewalk in front of the house.

Only on Saturdays did Anna Petrovich go out—with
her husband to the Queens apartment building, and to
do their weekly grocery shopping and other errands.

He never saw his parents kiss or hug, but Oliver
suspected that in their own way they loved each other.
Anna saved all of her affection for her son and never
held back showing it. Oliver wished that his father
would display just a fraction of the love and tender-
ness that came so easily to his mother. But his father
was awkward with any show of emotion and often accused his wife of babying and mollycoddling Oliver.

Oliver believed that, deep down, his father really
loved him and just had trouble showing it. But his
father's aloofness made him so nervous that for years
he couldn't decide whether to address him as Daddy,
Dad, or Father. Their contact was often so tense, and
Oliver was so frightened of using a title that would
offend his father, that he never called him anything at
all.

His parents never went out together like other cou-
ples on Long Island that he often saw. It never occurred to them just to pick up and go out to dinner or
to a movie. Although they lived in New York, their
minds were still in Yugoslavia. As a family, they rarely
went anywhere or did anything together. When Oliver

was younger they had traveled once to Yugoslavia to visit his father's parents, and he remembered an occasional family outing to Jones Beach or camping by a small lake in upstate New York. But those adventures were distant memories, and the only time they spent together anymore was at the Flushing apartment house or around their kitchen table, watching TV or eating dinner.

Oliver's mother, confined to the house with many hours to complete her few chores, had become progressively lazier. She often spent many hours watching television and drinking coffee, leaving the beds unmade until late afternoon, when she scrambled to get the house clean before her husband returned from work. At 5:30 when Svetozar Petrovich arrived home he expected the house to be immaculate, his bath drawn, and his dinner ready. One afternoon when Anna lost track of time working in her garden, she didn't have her husband's bath ready on time, and he beat her.

Oliver's parents didn't often fight because his mother never dared to talk back to his father. When his father's temper flared, often over the littlest things, there was nothing Oliver or his mother could do to stop him. He had seen his father furious because his mother hadn't washed a few dishes thoroughly enough, and another time because she had left the laundry on the living room couch. Once when she drank from a seltzer bottle and made slurping sounds, Svetozar got so angry that he called her a dumb roly-poly, and then hit her in the face. Oliver watched helplessly, knowing that if he interfered it would only exacerbate his father's temper.

The worst fight Oliver could remember between his

parents started when his mother stole twenty dollars out of his father's wallet because she needed something and had no spare money of her own. Oliver's father had automatically blamed him for the missing twenty dollars, reminding him of other times in the past when he had taken money.

"Oliver," he said with surprising calmness, "if you need money for anything, just ask me for it and I'll give it to you."

"But I didn't take it!" Oliver insisted. His denial got his father angry and he pushed Oliver for a confession.

"Leave him alone, Svetozar," his mother urged.

As Oliver went upstairs to his room he couldn't figure out what was going on. This time he was innocent and was worried that he was being framed. He was convinced that as his father was getting older he was also getting more out of control, and Oliver was ready to climb out of his window to escape his temper.

But before he could make a move he heard his father's heavy footsteps and Svetozar charged into the room brandishing the leg of a chair. His mother was right behind.

"Stop! Svetozar, Oliver didn't do it!" she cried. "I took the money. I'm sorry."

Unmoved by her tears, Oliver's father started to hit his wife while roaring, "How dare you! You almost made me kill my son!"

His mother fell to the ground and cried out to Oliver for help as her husband kept hitting her. Oliver saw that her nose was bleeding and she seemed to be bleeding from her arm and shoulder as well.

As always, he was immobilized watching his fa-

Anna and Svetozar Petrovich took great pride in their Great Neck home, and made sure the grounds were always manicured, the house well kept.

Facing the backyard was a screened-in porch; above were Oliver's bedroom and a guest room.

Svetozar's station wagon, parked in the driveway, was the car Oliver and Karlene used to discard the shotgun after the murder.

The living room of the Petrovich house.

Svetozar's shotgun, kept behind his bedroom door, was the weapon that Oliver used to kill his parents.

The Petrovich kitchen where Oliver and his parents were sitting when his mother told his father that Karlene had been living in their home.

On their porch, Anna and Svetozar served lunch to their guests, several hours before they were both killed.

Afraid to disobey his father's rules, Oliver never hung anything on his walls, and his bedroom was stark and always immaculate.

Karlene often spent many hours at a time hiding in Oliver's closet, crouching behind his clothes so as not to be discovered by his father.

The spare bedroom was also used by Oliver and Karlene, and was the room in which Oliver liked to study his police manual.

At his arraignment in the death of his parents in October 12, 1988, Oliver stood next to his attorney, Nicholas Marino. (© 1988 Dick Yarwood, Newsday)

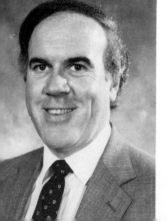

Daniel Cotter, Nassau County Assistant D.A., was the prosecuting attorney for the case of People versus Oliver Petrovich. (provided by Dan Cotter)

On March 16, 1989, from his seat in court, Oliver stared longingly at Karlene as she walked into the courtroom. (© 1989 Michael E. Ach, Newsday)

At Clinton Correctional Facility in Dannemora, New York, Oliver had a Polaroid picture taken to send to his Angel. (photo provided by Oliver Petrovich)

ther's rage. But suddenly fear for his mother's safety propelled him into motion.

"Stop!" he shouted. "That's enough! You're gonna k-k-ill her!"

As if waking from a trance, Oliver's father finally stopped.

The next day Anna's body was black and blue, but nobody mentioned the incident and it was as if it had never happened.

When Oliver came home from work early that afternoon the only thing out of the ordinary was his mother's mood. She yelled at him for spilling a drink on the table, and got unusually upset with him for running the water so hard that it splashed on the kitchen floor. Anna was still bickering with Oliver when Svetozar arrived home from work, but he didn't seem to notice. Tired and hungry, he had only one thing on his mind. "Anna, is my bath ready?" he asked.

She nodded as she hurried to the linen closet to get him a towel.

As he had done so many other times through the years, Oliver looked at his two parents and felt all alone.

Chapter 13:

SEPTEMBER 25, 1988

"I'LL TELL YOU THE TRUTH"

Oliver had never before felt so frightened or alone. He sat in a small interview room, eight feet square, with a desk, two chairs, and a filing cabinet. There were three solid walls and a front wall with a door and a large glass window that looked into the main squad room.

After some time sitting by himself, the door opened and Detective Parpan walked in. He was a tall, imposing man, but with a kind face, Oliver thought. Still standing, Detective Parpan asked Oliver if he was hungry or wanted coffee. Oliver nodded, and he sent for coffee and a doughnut.

Once seated across the table from Oliver, the detective asked him the routine questions of identification. After taking the necessary preliminary information he tried to initiate a conversation. "How long have you lived in Great Neck, Oliver?"

"Since 1984." Oliver looked down at the table as he answered.

"What do you like to do in your spare time?"

"Work on cars."

"Interesting," Detective Parpan responded. "My car has a rear axle oil leak. Do you know if it's hard to change an oil seal at the rear axle?"

Oliver mumbled a response that the detective had trouble hearing. Then more clearly he added, "I also want to become a police officer. I even bought a wrecked police car."

Detective Parpan nodded to indicate his interest.

"Oliver," he continued, "do you know of any enemies that your father might have?"

"No."

"Are you aware of any valuables in the house?"

He shook his head.

"What about weapons?" Detective Parpan asked.

"I know my f-father keeps a loaded shotgun in his bedroom. And he has other weapons that he uses for hunting."

"Oliver, what was the relationship like between Karlene and your parents?"

"My m-m-mom really likes her." For the first time his eyes started to light up. "My father likes her but he's not crazy about her. He knows she's been living at the house on weekends but n-not d-during the week."

Detective Parpan paused for a moment, then resumed his questioning. "Oliver, I want you to tell me everything that happened yesterday."

For the next two hours Oliver answered the same questions he had already answered in the police car. But while he repeated the same planned answers, his mind kept wandering to his Angel, who was being questioned in the adjacent room by a female detective, Ronda Milgrim.

During Oliver's interrogation Detective Parpan left the room several times to confer with the detective next door. Each time he returned Oliver asked him about Karlene, how she was feeling and how she was doing.

After a few trips back and forth Detective Parpan was expecting Oliver's same questions about his Angel, but was surprised to hear him ask instead, "How bad are my parents?"

Detective Parpan sat down and looked across at Oliver. "I'm sorry, Oliver," he said gently. "I thought you already knew. Your parents are dead."

"I thought so," Oliver answered, "because the ambulances didn't leave right away."

The questions continued and the stories that Oliver and Karlene gave were so identical, down to the finest details, that it troubled Detective Parpan. But there were two discrepancies that bothered him even more.

In Oliver's first version he had said that he had walked down the driveway to the back of the house and looked in the kitchen window. But now he was adamant that he'd never walked down the driveway, yet in Karlene's story they had. He also insisted that his parents liked Karlene and knew about their living arrangements, but Karlene told Detective Milgrim that Oliver's parents hated her and his father had threatened several times to kill her.

For the first time since he answered his phone in the middle of the night, Brian Parpan began to suspect that Oliver was lying, and he decided that he'd better talk to him about his concerns. The time was 10:30 A.M.

"Oliver," he said, in their same positions across from each other at the table, "I'm having some problems that are troubling me. There are discrepancies that I think are important. And before I continue questioning you, I'm going to give you your rights."

Oliver just stared straight ahead.

Detective Parpan proceeded. "You have the right to remain silent. You don't have to speak to me anymore. Any statements that you do make will be used against you in court."

Oliver still did not react.

"Oliver, do you understand that you don't have to talk to me anymore?"

"Yes."

"You have a right to have an attorney present before answering any questions, or at any time. Do you understand?"

"Yes," Oliver answered.

"If you can't afford to hire a lawyer, one will be provided free of charge. And you have a right to remain silent until you have a chance to speak with that attorney. Do you understand?"

Oliver answered, still not looking at the detective, "Yes, it's like on TV. I've seen this on TV."

"Do you understand these rights?" Detective Parpan asked him again.

"Yes."

"With these rights in mind, are you still willing to speak with me about what you did prior to and afterward, and about the overall incident?"

Oliver finally looked at the detective. "Yes, no problem," he answered.

"Oliver, there are two problems that are really bothering me. The first thing that bothers me is the kind of relationship you and Karlene had with your father. You have indicated that everything was just fine between you and your father and between Karlene and your father, but from what Karlene has said, things were far from fine in your house. She told us that she had been living in your house and hiding in your room, and that your mother was helpful but your father knew nothing about your living arrangement. And that your father hated her guts."

Oliver gave no sign of interest, but Detective Parpan continued to look right at him and kept talking. "The second problem I'm having is whether you looked in the kitchen window, which first you said you did, and then you said you didn't, but Karlene told us that you did walk down the driveway. If you did look in that window, you would surely have seen your mother's body."

Oliver looked up and said, "Maybe we did walk to the back of the house with John, but we never went to the kitchen window."

At that moment Detective Donnelly entered the room, and the two detectives stepped outside for a conference.

"Anything new at the scene?" Parpan asked Donnelly, who had just been in radio contact with another detective still at the Great Neck house.

"No, nothing."

"I just gave him his rights because of the discrepancies in their stories," Parpan said as they started to walk back into the room where Oliver waited.

Inside the room the questioning continued with both detectives. Donnelly said, "Oliver, you've already said that you went to the back of the house by the window."

"M-maybe I walked to the b-back, but not by the window," he answered.

"Oliver," continued Parpan, "we think you're lying."

On cue Donnelly added, "We understand your problem with your father, but why your mother?"

"You're lying to me!" Oliver shouted abruptly. "I know Karlene is not telling you these things. You're trying to trick me!"

Ignoring his outburst Donnelly asked calmly, "Oliver, your father didn't know about your relationship with Karlene?"

"Oh yes, my father knew." Oliver was calmer again, looking down at his hands on the table.

"Did you go to the back of the house?" Donnelly asked again.

"No."

"Even Karlene has told us that you went to the back of the house."

"Oh no," Oliver answered. "That's not true. She couldn't have told you that. I didn't go down the driveway to the back of the house."

Donnelly was getting impatient. "Do you know, Oliver, I can't understand this. I can understand your having all those problems with your father, but I can't understand why you did it to your mother. Why your mother, Oliver? Your mother was taking care of you all this time. Karlene told us your mother had been going along with your plan, hiding her and taking care of her. That's what she told the detective. Why your mother?" He was shouting now.

Oliver didn't answer. Almost a minute passed before he finally looked up but remained silent.

Detective Parpan took over. "Oliver, it's only a matter of time before everyone in the seat you're in starts talking. Sooner or later, everyone who sits in your chair in this room starts talking. It may take hours, or even days, but eventually you'll get sick and tired of sitting here." He looked into Oliver's unresponsive eyes.

"Oliver, did you ever hear of an old saying, 'It was the straw that broke the camel's back?' "

No response.

"Oliver, something your mother did had to be equivalent to putting the straw on the camel's back, that caused you to do what you did."

The detectives left the room to confer outside. They realized that they were on borrowed time and every minute was critical to their interrogation. Once an attorney was summoned to represent Oliver, all questioning would have to stop.

When they heard the phone ring in the main squad room, they both jumped.

"That neighbor, John Lambert, may have called a lawyer for Oliver," Parpan said to Donnelly.

Waiting tensely to hear who was on the phone, they were relieved to find that the call was not for them.

They agreed that they were close to a confession, and needed to pull a final trump card to break Oliver.

"What do you think about bringing the girl in?" Parpan suggested.

From their experience in homicide interrogations, they knew that putting two suspects together was a risk, but after almost five hours of questioning they were both exhausted, frustrated, and willing to take the chance.

"We'll keep it controlled and hope for the best," Parpan said as they walked back into the room where Oliver waited.

Detective Donnelly spoke first. "Oliver, if I bring Karlene in here and she looks you in the eye and says that you're lying about going down the driveway and going to the back of the house, would you tell us the truth?"

Without looking up Oliver answered, "If she says that, then I'll tell you the truth."

In the adjacent room Karlene was still being questioned about her relationship with Oliver and his parents, and about the events of the preceding day. She was telling Detective Milgrim how much she and Oliver loved each other, and that they were planning to get married, when Detective Donnelly walked into the room.

"How is Oliver?" Karlene immediately asked him. "Can I see him?"

"No," Donnelly answered curtly. "Oliver isn't telling us anything." He looked at her with a more kindly expression. "Karlene, if you tell us what really happened, we can help Oliver. You're the only person who can help, if you tell us the truth."

Detective Milgrim followed his lead. "Karlene," she urged gently, "I promise if you tell us the truth, if Oliver did do it, he'll go to a psychiatric hospital to get help."

"It's up to you to help," Donnelly repeated.

Karlene remained silent, staring at her hands while picking at her fingernails.

Suddenly, an abrupt change in Donnelly's tone made her snap to attention. "What the hell is the matter with you?" he yelled. "If you think you're going to walk out of here and live some kind of fairy-tale life, you're wrong! You don't really want to help Oliver." As quickly as his anger had emerged it receded, and his voice became gentle again. "You're the only person who can do it, if you tell us exactly what happened."

Detective Milgrim took her hands. "Look at my face, Karlene," she said softly. "I'm your friend. You can trust me. I won't hurt you. I wouldn't lie to you." She squeezed her hand. "You can believe me." She held Karlene's eyes with her own. "Oliver is not a murderer; he's a sick man," Milgrim said. "If that's the truth he won't go to jail but to a psychiatric hospital."

After a long lapse Karlene spoke, in a voice that was almost a whisper. "Do you swear to God?"

"I promised you I wouldn't lie to you," Milgrim answered. "I'm your friend."

"Are you just saying this now and then later he's going to be in jail?" Karlene asked meekly.

"No," Milgrim answered. "I never go back on my word."

Detective Donnelly intervened. "Karlene, we're going to take you to another room to see Oliver. We want you to hold his hands, look him in the eyes, and tell him that he's lying about not going down the driveway to the back of the house, because you were there with him." He waited for a reaction but she just continued to stare at him. "Karlene," he repeated, "is that true?"

"Yes," she answered. "We did go down the driveway to the back of the house."

"Then all I want you to do is look him straight in the eyes and tell him that he's lying and that he did go to the back of the house, because you were with him. Nothing else. No kissing, no talking about anything else, or we'll pull you right out of the room."

"Okay, I will," she said.

Before going to see Oliver, Karlene asked to use the ladies' room. Detective Milgrim accompanied her there.

"You really love Oliver, don't you?" she asked while waiting.

"He is the kindest person I ever met," Karlene answered. "He loves me, he looks after me, and he gives me everything I ask for. He'd do anything to make me happy because he knows how my childhood days were and that I was never a happy child." She wiped away a tear. "So he goes out of his way to be my mother and my father—you know, to make me happy."

Detective Milgrim gave her a quick hug. "I'm your friend, Karlene," she said. "I'll never hurt either of you."

Karlene was then escorted into Oliver's interview room. She sat down on a chair that had been brought in and placed next to his. She reached over to him, held his hand and said softly, "Oliver, you know you walked down that driveway to the back of the house, because I was with you."

"No I didn't," Oliver mumbled.

"Tell them the truth, Oliver," Karlene persisted. "I was with you and I already told them you did. Tell them the truth." She started to cry. "It's okay, Oliver." She patted his arm.

Oliver looked back into her eyes. "Angel, don't believe them. They're lying. They're trying to trick you."

Just then Detective Milgrim took Karlene's arm to signal that their talk was over, and guided her out of the room.

"Oliver," Detective Donnelly said, "you told us you were going to tell us the truth if she came in and looked you in the eye and said you definitely went down the driveway. Well, now I want to hear the truth."

Oliver stared blankly ahead.

"Come on, Oliver," Donnelly persisted. "I still want to know why you included your mother in this. Your father was the one that was giving you all the trouble. Your mother was helping you through this whole thing."

"Oliver," Detective Parpan added, "if you don't tell us the truth we're going to find out our way, so you might as well make it easier on all of us."

"You did very good, Karlene," Detective Milgrim assured her when they were back in the other room.

"Will Oliver go to jail?" Karlene asked again, still teary-eyed.

"No."

With no warning, Karlene's crying became more intense until she was sobbing.

"What's wrong, Karlene?" Milgrim asked. "There's something wrong."

"Yes!" she cried. "Oliver did it! He killed his parents!" Still sobbing, she told the sympathetic detective the whole story. When she finished she asked for a pen and paper, and scribbled a note to Oliver. "Don't worry about anything," she wrote. "You'll be okay. I love you. You're going to be home with me very soon because a police officer told me. You can trust them. They won't hurt you."

Karlene asked Detective Milgrim to give the note to Oliver, and she promised that she would.

From the window of Oliver's interview room Detective Donnelly looked out on the main squad room and saw Milgrim waving her arms and motioning him to come out. He left the room and hurried toward her. She started to talk so fast he could barely understand her.

"She just told me!" Milgrim exclaimed. "Karlene! She was in the house when he did it!"

Donnelly went immediately into the room where Karlene was still weeping. "You were in the house when he did it?" he asked.

"Yes," she cried.

"What did you do with the gun?" he asked.

"He threw it off the Throgs Neck Bridge."

"Okay."

Milgrim continued to console Karlene while Donnelly walked back into Oliver's interview room where he and Detective Parpan were still sitting. He took the chair across from Oliver. "Oliver," he said firmly,

"I'm going to say one thing to you: Throgs Neck Bridge."

Abruptly Oliver rolled his head back up against the wall and said, "She told you."

"Okay, Oliver," Detective Donnelly said, "let's have the truth."

Oliver sat there for almost a minute, finally looked up at the detective and said, "Well, I'm trying to figure out how I'm going to tell you."

"Start from the beginning, Oliver," Donnelly said. "Start from wherever you want."

He started to cry.

"That's right, cry, Oliver," Donnelly said. "It's good for you."

Slowly Oliver began to talk. "Well, you know, my f-father, he's a racist. He should of belonged to the KKK. He hated blacks. He hated my g-girlfriend. He caught me one time going out of the house and he told me he was going to shoot me if I continued going out with blacks." He was crying freely now, and trying to wipe away his tears as he continued speaking. "I thought my m-mother was helping me. But my mother turned me in to him, and I think she was a racist too." He put his head down on the table, then lifted it again. "They've tormented me, tormented me. All I wanted to do was to have a relationship with this girl and they said it was no g-good. They say no good."

As if a new thought had entered his mind, he said, "These people that came over to the house yesterday . . . yeah, I went to the store for my father. And these people came over. Phil and his wife came over. There was supposed to be another couple coming over. They had a nineteen-year-old daughter. They're trying to set me up with a nineteen-year-old white girl. I don't want to go out with a nineteen-year-old white girl. I wanted to go out with this girl. I met her back in April and I liked going out with her.

"You know, I've been thinking about this. I thought a couple of times about how to kill him. All I want to do, is if I kill them, I can just live in the house. I thought about my father owning the apartment building. On occasion we would go there. I thought maybe I could do them in in the basement of the apartment building and make it look like a robbery. So I went to a co-worker, a buddy named Vinnie, to get a gun and a silencer. I thought that maybe I could club them to death and put them in the car and burn the car up. I didn't know what to do, but I knew I was going to kill them.

"On this day it just got to be that I knew I had to kill them. But I knew Karlene could not stay in the house that day because of all these people coming over. Karlene used to stay in the closet all the time. We used to put her in the closet when there was any problems going on. I knew there was people going to be in the house all day. There was no way I was going to ask her to stay in the closet all day. So I told her to go see her sister, and she took off. I said come on back later in the evening, go to the spot at the side of the house, you know, I'll be looking for you." And Oliver proceeded to tell them the rest of the events as they had actually taken place.

When he finished, Detective Parpan said, "Oliver, we need a statement so we can charge you fairly."

"What am I being charged with?" he asked.

Parpan, knowing that in New York State the charge of first-degree murder could only be given for killing a police or other peace officer, answered Oliver slowly. "The top charge," he said. "Second-degree murder."

By 4 P.M. Oliver had written his confession statement and signed each page. A little later, guided by Detective Parpan, he made a videotaped confession. "Make sure you say that we read you your rights, and that you understood them," the detective told him.

After giving the detectives such a hard time Oliver wanted to please them, and he did just as he had been instructed.

Afterward, Parpan went to speak to Karlene. "Do you have a place to go?" he asked her.

"No," she answered timidly.

"Would your mother take you in?"

"No," she repeated.

Parpan made arrangements for her to stay overnight in a shelter, where Karlene waited to hear which psychiatric hospital Oliver was going to be sent to so she could visit him.

Two days later, while watching television, Karlene heard on the news that Oliver had been taken to the Nassau County Jail.

Chapter 14:
SEPTEMBER 28, 1988
"THAT'S THE BIGGEST CROCK OF SHIT"

Nicholas A. Marino first met Oliver Petrovich three days after he had been charged with second-degree murder.

As a member of the Major Felony Panel of the Assigned Counsel Defender Plan, he was one of seventy-three private attorneys in Nassau County assigned on a rotating basis to defend indigent persons arrested for major felonies.

Marino was thirty-two years old and had worked for

five years as a district attorney in the Bronx before deciding to go into private practice on Long Island where he lived. He had recently been made partner in Parola, Feuerstein & Gross, a small but well-established law firm in Wantagh, on the south shore of the Island.

Having been notified that he was Assigned Counsel for the day, Marino had reported to District Court Part 9 in Mineola, where the judge informed him that the defendant was Oliver Petrovich.

He remembered seeing the story in *Newsday*, but was not familiar with many of the details.

"I'll understand if you don't want this case," the judge told him. "I won't force you to take it."

As Marino faced the judge he wavered momentarily. He was thinking about his already hectic schedule and heavy case load, the added pressure this case would create for him, the press and media coverage that would unquestionably follow. And he was wondering what his decision would mean to his own future. He looked at the judge, who was waiting for his decision.

"I'll take it," he said.

An hour later Marino was in the holding area of the Nassau County Jail when Oliver's name was called. Dressed in the bright orange county jail uniform, Oliver approached and took a seat on a bench across from him. They were separated by metal bars.

Right away Marino sensed that Oliver didn't like him. His eyes were cold and vacant, and he refused to look at him.

"Good morning," Marino said. "My name is Nick Marino, and I've been assigned by the courts to represent you."

Oliver still wouldn't look at him. "What does that m-mean?" he asked.

"It means that I'll be visiting you in jail and working with you to prepare your defense for your trial, which may not begin for months."

Oliver had been warned by several inmates not to trust any free lawyers, that they wouldn't look out for him but would only try to make deals that would best serve themselves. He finally looked the lawyer in the eye.

Nick Marino had dark hair and a full dark beard that made Oliver even more nervous. He didn't trust himself to speak because he knew he wouldn't be able to control his stuttering.

They met that morning for about an hour. Marino asked a lot of questions and Oliver answered them as briefly as possible. Marino could see that Oliver was tense, and while he wasn't sure whether Oliver was lying to him, he was certain that he was holding back.

The next day they spent two hours together, and Oliver changed many of the details of his story from the day before. Marino was frustrated but decided that patience was his best approach. Oliver still didn't look at him during their meetings and his stuttering seemed to have gotten even worse.

Marino had been informed that one of Oliver's aunts was considering hiring a private lawyer and he was annoyed at the thought that he might be wasting his time. But still he came every day to talk to Oliver and to draw from him as much information as possible. He asked Oliver questions about his childhood, his parents, his girlfriend Karlene Francis, the night of the murder, the cover-up, the police interrogation, and his confession. The answers Oliver gave were limited and continued to vary from day to day. Finally Marino felt himself running out of patience.

"What is it, Oliver?" he demanded. "You're not being honest with me. How can I help you if you keep lying to me?"

At last Oliver looked at Marino's face, and he told him about the serious warnings he had gotten from other inmates about court-appointed lawyers.

As he listened, Marino's face turned progressively redder, until he finally exploded. "Oliver, that's the biggest crock of shit I ever heard!"

For the first time since they had met Oliver smiled, and Marino had his first glimmer of hope that they had made a small dent in the wall between them.

After that Oliver began to look forward to Marino's visits and to talk to him about everything on his mind. His answers finally became consistent and as Marino started to believe that Oliver was telling him the truth, their meetings grew longer.

Marino reviewed Oliver's past arrest record, and Oliver told him briefly about each of the three incidents listed on his arrest sheet.

They had all occurred in 1985 when Oliver was twenty years old. For his first violation, illegal possession of a vehicle and altered ID number on the license plates, Oliver had pleaded guilty to a Class A misdemeanor, and had been placed on conditional probation.

Several months later, a charge of vehicular assault and criminal mischief had been treated as a traffic violation, and he had been fined $150.

In the third charge, for possession of a stolen car, Oliver had been convicted of disorderly conduct and released on "conditional discharge."

The assault case, for which Oliver had been sent to a psychologist, was not listed on his record, nor were several other car-related incidents that Oliver described to Marino.

As they talked, Oliver became more willing to tell Marino about his racist parents, how his father had abused him and his mother had betrayed him. Finally he confided in Marino all about the furious battle he had had within himself the night he killed his parents.

"I started to breathe deep and fast, and felt like my heart was about to explode," he said. "My mind was battling my heart, and the war was bringing my gut feelings right up to my throat. My throat started to close up and I felt like I was standing on my head. Finally my mind decided to save my heart, and that's when there were no more doubts. The only doubt was could I do it fast enough."

It was difficult for Oliver to talk about the night of the murder, but he liked to talk about his relationship with Angel, and about his car, the only other object of his love. As he grew more comfortable with Marino, Oliver started to have questions of his own.

"Why are you asking this?" he asked in response to one of Marino's questions. "Why are you doing this?" he often wondered aloud. Or "What does that mean?"

From the moment Oliver had decided to trust his court-appointed lawyer, he became totally cooperative with Marino and willing to accept his advice and suggestions. Many times Oliver called Marino collect at his office from jail, to inform him of a new detail that he had remembered or a point he thought was important.

Oliver's faith and confidence in Marino continued to grow over the year between their first meeting and his

trial. By the time the trial finally started, Oliver was
certain that Marino could make any jury believe anything, and that he could definitely convince a jury that
he, Oliver Petrovich, was insane.

But the longer Nick Marino knew Oliver Petrovich,
the more confused he felt. Over and over again after
their meetings he reviewed his notes, thought about
their conversations, and asked himself, What makes
Oliver Petrovich tick?

Beginning to prepare for the trial, Marino decided
that it was vital to retain a psychologist who could
help him learn more about his client.

Chapter 15:
NOVEMBER 10, 1988
"PLEASE GET ME OUT OF HERE"

As Oliver woke up he was having a dream that it was time to get up and go to work. "Come on, Angel," he muttered, still half asleep. Then he opened his eyes and saw the bars of his jail cell.

The weeks since he arrived had passed in a blur. Oliver knew that his parents had been buried in a cemetery in Port Washington, a neighboring town to Great Neck. He vaguely remembered his cousin Terry telling him that his aunt and uncle had taken a bank loan to pay for the funeral.

Oliver had thought about putting in a request to the

warden for permission to attend his parents' funeral. But when he pictured the scene—his relatives crying over the two coffins, while he stood nearby handcuffed and guarded by several police officers—he changed his mind. The image in his head made him feel so ashamed that Oliver knew he couldn't face his family.

On this November morning after breakfast Oliver picked up the pen and a sheet of paper that he had managed to persuade a sympathetic prison guard to give him. Sitting on his bed he leaned forward, and with the paper on his lap began to write the letter:

Dear Tatoe,

It's me Oliver writing you, I hope your fine and Mama too. I think I'd had enough time in jail and I want to come home, but I'm sorry about the air cleaner on my car, but I'll never take it off again and I won't buy anymore of those tires that you don't like, if you'll just get me out of here. I know I was bad about this, I promise, Tatoe, that I'll help you cut the grass and go to Flushing with you on Saturdays. I definitely will sweep the floors from the roof down to the first floor and change washers in all of the apartments or I mean whoever needs it. But I know the real reason I mean the garage, I always used to throw tools anywhere I wanted to and leave motor oil laying around in those oil pans open and made the garage smell like an auto shop. It won't never be that way again and I will start saving up my money and open a savings account in your bank. I promise I won't rev-up, I mean I won't cream my car motor very high no more, I know you used to hate it so much and yell out the window all the time about it at me, the people hated it too and it was bad for the motor too and I won't use straight

60 motor oil. I realize it was too heavy an oil for the motor. I'm gonna stop the oil leak in my car, that's the first thing I will do is jack up the front and drop the oil pan and order a new oil pan from Chrysler.

You know that black-girl-bitch, she is going back to her galaxy and she will not control anymore, I promise you, Tatoe. Just please get me out of here, the people in here are robbing me every day, and they talk too much, I cannot sleep good anymore, and the food is rotten, and it's never enough, I'm starving to death in here day and night. And don't worry, Tatoe, I have not told anyone about the Power.

Thank you Tatoe
Sincerely Oliver Petrovich

Oliver then folded the letter, addressed the envelope to Svetozar Petrovich at 64 Richard Avenue in Great Neck, and asked the prison guard to mail it for him.

Chapter 16:
NOVEMBER 16, 1988
"HE HAS SO LITTLE AND WANTS SO MUCH"

Nick Marino happened to be at the Nassau County Correctional Facility on the morning that Alan Klein first came to meet Oliver. When Marino saw Dr. Klein waiting in the attorney conference area, they agreed that it would be a good idea for Marino to introduce the two men.

Oliver was escorted down the corridor into the tiny conference room where they both waited for him. "Oliver," Marino said, "I want you to meet Dr. Klein."

Dr. Klein held out his hand and Oliver shook it limply.

"He's a friend, Oliver," Marino said. "A good guy. I'd like you to talk to him."

When Oliver showed no reaction, Marino decided that it would be best if he left.

"Good morning, Oliver," Dr. Klein greeted him. "I'm a psychologist and I've been retained by Nick Marino to talk to you and to do a psychological evaluation."

Oliver sat across from him at a scarred gray metal table that had been used many times over the years by prisoners talking to their attorneys.

"Oliver, do you know who Nick Marino is?"

"Yes, he's my attorney." He spoke in a monotone and still looked down.

"I've been asked by your attorney to perform a psychological evaluation. Have you ever undergone a psychological evaluation before?"

"No."

Dr. Klein tried to explain, in brief and simple terms, what a psychological evaluation consisted of. "I'll be spending time with you," he said, "talking about your background and other things. Then I'll be administering several psychological tests and I will request your cooperation in the administering of these tests." He watched Oliver for a reaction but still saw none and noticed that he seemed listless. "Oliver," he continued, "the information you share will remain under attorney/client privilege until it is called into court. My role is to get as good an understanding of your personality as possible." Still looking at him, Dr. Klein paused for a response.

"I understand," Oliver said.

"Oliver," Dr. Klein continued, "do you understand what the term 'confidentiality' means?"

"Not really."

Again Dr. Klein explained it as simply as he thought appropriate.

"Okay," Oliver responded. "I understand."

"Oliver, where did you live before being sent here?"

Dr. Klein proceeded to ask him a series of questions to determine his awareness of reality and how much he understood. He was trying to assess whether he was competent to consent to a psychological evaluation, and whether he would be competent to participate in his own defense. They sat facing each other at the table in the small room, with the only light coming from a ceiling fixture overhead.

He started with simple questions. "What is your phone number?" "What is your date of birth?" "Who is your attorney?"

As Dr. Klein progressed, the questions became more complex and required more thought. "What is the role of a judge?" "A D.A.?" "A jury?" "What does it mean to plead guilty?" "Innocent?" "What will happen if you are convicted of this crime?"

Dr. Klein observed that Oliver answered in a straightforward manner, but his responses were limited and his mood seemed depressed. When they were discussing the pending charges Oliver told him, "I face fifty to life, you know. The D.A. and the jury will be looking to give me the maximum of fifty years, but I'd like to get out of jail in fifteen years or less."

"Oliver, do you trust Mr. Marino?" Dr. Klein asked.

He shrugged his shoulders. "Well, some of the inmates told m-me not to trust him, that I should work on m-my own defense." He paused, then added, "You know, he's court-appointed."

Dr. Klein continued to periodically change the focus of their conversation and watch for Oliver's responses. "Oliver, how did you feel when you made the confession?" he asked.

"Depressed."

"Have you considered suicide?"

"Yes."

"Have you tried suicide?"

"No," Oliver answered slowly.

On their second meeting Dr. Klein observed that Oliver seemed friendlier and more relaxed. He was willing to talk about his family and background, and when Klein asked him questions he answered with less hesitation.

When they discussed his grades in school Oliver told him that his grades were mostly in the seventies and eighties—passing, but not exceptional. He had repeated one year of school, transferring to Automotive High School in Brooklyn, but it was too hard to travel so far carrying so many heavy tools, so he dropped out and never graduated.

They talked about his job at Pepsi, about his interest in becoming a police officer, about the few occasions he had been arrested, about the girls he had dated.

"I never had a problem meeting girls," Oliver admitted. "A lot of times I went to shopping malls and watched the girls go by until I saw one that I liked."

"Oliver, tell me about Karlene," Dr. Klein said, still trying to look him in the eye.

For the first time Oliver lit up, as he told the psychologist how much he loved his Angel and how they wanted to get married.

"Has Angel come to visit you?" Dr. Klein asked.

"She did in the beginning but it's hard for her to get here." His head dropped again and all eye contact disappeared.

The only other time Dr. Klein saw any animation from Oliver was when he talked about his cars. He remembered everything about every car he ever owned and discussed his latest police cruiser with explicit details. He told Dr. Klein about chasing cars on the parkway, driving fast and crazy, and pretending to be a highway cop.

His enthusiasm disappeared instantly when Dr. Klein diverted the conversation to the subject of Oliver's parents.

"Oliver, tell me about your father."

"He was very s-strict," he answered slowly. "He was always complaining that m-my cars were littering the driveway." He hesitated, then said, "All I really wanted to do was prove to m-my f-father that I knew what I was doing." His head dropped even lower. "He made f-fun of me and tormented me every day." Suddenly Oliver looked as if he were about to smile. "But then he went and made special tools for me for my car," he said.

"How did he torment you, Oliver?" Dr. Klein asked.

"He would s-say things to hurt me," he answered. And he was against m-me going out with black and Spanish girls. B-but I didn't like white girls. B-black and Spanish girls were nicer and p-prettier. And American girls had an attitude p-problem. Black and Spanish girls had a b-better attitude."

"What do you mean by better attitude?"

"They were easier to talk to," he answered thoughtfully. "White girls cursed a lot. Angel had no attitude problem."

During his interview of almost three hours Alan Klein took many pages of notes. He observed that Oliver, in his responses, usually muttered or mumbled, and often stuttered. His affect was flat, with no display of anger or emotion. With his head usually down and virtually no eye contact, he presented himself as almost suicidal.

Oliver had, in fact, just been transferred out of an observation tier in the prison, where he had been watched for a possible suicide attempt.

Oliver's stories continued to change, Dr. Klein observed. In one conversation he contradicted himself several times and created different scenarios that he apparently had discussed with other jailmates. The only consistency was his love for Karlene Francis. Their relationship was obsessional in nature and outweighed all other considerations.

When Oliver talked about his father he seemed emotionally detached, Dr. Klein noted. He desperately wanted his father's approval, but his father always put him down, which gave him great pain. He talked about anger toward his father, fear of his father, and how he missed his father and wished he were still here. The only time Oliver showed any emotion was when he told Dr. Klein that he had recently been calling his house in Great Neck, pretending to himself that one of his parents would answer the phone and everything would be okay.

Dr. Klein later told Nick Marino that Oliver never

seemed to understand how serious the consequences were to the kind of action he had taken.

As he left the Nassau County Correctional Facility, Alan Klein was thinking about his final conversation with Oliver that day.

"Oliver, what do you feel about your future?" he had asked.

"I feel good about it," Oliver had answered. "I want a second chance with Angel. I'm hoping I just get ten to fifteen years. Whatever I get out of jail will be helpful to my future."

On his third meeting with Oliver, Dr. Klein was prepared to begin the psychological testing. The process was not new for him, as he had administered hundreds of psychological tests, had worked with elementary school and college students, and with patients with a wide variety of emotional disorders. A diplomate in forensic psychology, Alan Klein had been in private practice since 1971. He had carefully chosen five tests, each commonly used in psychological evaluations, that he thought would reveal an accurate pattern of behavior. No single test would mean anything in and of itself, but in combination they would present a better picture of Oliver.

The tests he used were the Wechsler Adult Intelligence Scale–Revised, Minnesota Multiphasic Personality Inventory, Rorschach Psychodiagnostic Test, Bender Visual Motor Gestalt Test, and Human Figure Drawings.

"Good morning, Oliver," Dr. Klein greeted him, and again received a limp handshake and minimal eye contact. "Did you get enough sleep last night?"

"Yes."

"Did you have enough to eat?"

"Yes."

As he had proceeded over the three preliminary sessions, Dr. Klein explained each test to Oliver.

The Wechsler Intelligence Scale, more commonly known as an IQ test, is a standardized, objective, individually administered intelligence test. There are two major parts. The verbal part draws on a number of areas of intellectual ability by asking a variety of questions which are responded to verbally. It requires recall of information that reflects an individual's awareness of the world around him and how much he has benefited from his past educational and life experiences.

After administering the tests, Dr. Klein calculated Oliver's verbal IQ score to be 79, which is considerably less than average. By New York State education laws, a score of 75 would be the upper limit of the educable mentally retarded range. A score of 79, Dr. Klein explained, would impose severe limitations in functioning, in understanding and dealing with relationships, understanding situations, and in being able to formulate accurate judgments regarding relationships between various facets of experience.

Oliver's score of 112 on the nonverbal, or performance part of the IQ test was above average and reflected his ability to deal with objects and things. The test consists of various problem-solving activities, including putting block patterns together, assembling puzzles, and responding to pictures, all of which Oliver did obediently and without questions.

In Dr. Klein's judgment, a discrepancy of 33 points between Oliver's two scores on the IQ test showed a very uneven level of functioning. To attempt to put them together and say that his overall functioning was average would be completely inaccurate, he said.

Throughout the entire evaluation process Dr. Klein was surprised that Oliver never asked about the tests. Unlike most people, Oliver showed no curiosity over how he had scored and never even asked, "Am I crazy?" He showed no expression, but passively accepted whatever he was told to do.

When he concluded the various tests Dr. Klein told Marino that his clinical impressions, combined with test results, showed an individual with severe emotional problems who was unable to cope with emotional stress.

"He doesn't function well in verbal reasoning," Klein explained to Marino, "and has only limited insight in the understanding of situations."

Based on his evaluation, Dr. Klein felt that Oliver's appreciation of his waiver of his Miranda rights would have been extremely limited, and that he had no understanding of what his actions would mean at some indefinite time in the future.

"Nick," he concluded, "look at how he responded when asked if he understood. He said, 'Yeah, it's just like on TV.'"

After reviewing Oliver's videotaped confession, his written statements, police officers' notes and letters Oliver had written, Dr. Klein told Marino that he had seen many sides of Oliver.

"I believe that Oliver is incapable of forming any warm attachments that we define as love," he said. "He sees people as objects to possess and use and, in turn, to be possessed by." He explained to Marino,

"Oliver has no insight or understanding of himself, Nick, and unfortunately, he has no conscience."

As he closed his notes and stood up, he looked at Marino and said, "The saddest part about Oliver is that he sees himself as having so little, and wanting so much."

Chapter 17:
FEBRUARY–JULY 1989
"WE'RE PREPARED TO GO TO TRIAL"

On the Monday morning after Oliver was charged with second-degree murder, Daniel Cotter, Assistant D.A., was assigned to prosecute the case. Having been in the D.A.'s office since 1973, Cotter had been assigned to the Major Offense Bureau and the majority of the cases he handled were major felonies, homicides, and robberies.

At forty-two, Cotter was a large man—about six feet tall, heavyset, with a receding hairline, brown, piercing eyes, and a commanding presence. Within the D.A.'s office, whenever his name came up, the consensus among other assistant D.A.'s and colleagues was, "Dan Cotter? He's the best."

When he reviewed the Petrovich case, Cotter was not overly concerned. There was plenty of evidence that Oliver Petrovich had indeed committed the murders. From his experience he figured that at the trial the key question would be whether it was intentional murder or an act of extreme emotional disturbance. The jury's decision would mean the difference between a verdict of murder or manslaughter.

During the following few months in the Nassau County Jail, Oliver's depression deepened. The only thing he looked forward to was visits from his Angel. Every day he waited for her and desperately hoped that she'd show up.

"Oliver," she cried to him during one of her first visits, "they promised me they'd help us. I swear, they tricked me into persuading you to confess. They told me you'd go to a psychiatric hospital if I cooperated. Oh God, Oliver, they went back on their word. What are we going to do?"

Soon afterward, when she was having a problem with housing and didn't know where she'd be able to live, Oliver remembered how kind Detective Parpan had been to him during his interrogation, and on a whim called him collect and asked him to please help his Angel.

On two occasions Parpan sent police officers to the location where Karlene was living, to try to offer her assistance. But about a month later when Oliver called the detective late at night at his home, Parpan ran out of both patience and kindness.

"No," he snapped into the phone. "I don't accept collect calls at home."

Karlene's visits to Oliver, which at first were about twice a week, soon began to taper off. The trips were difficult for her, and over the next few months dwindled to occasional appearances. Oliver, in turn, withdrew even further into himself.

His only steady visitor was Nick Marino, his attorney, who came to the jail several times a week to see him. With little else to think about, Oliver cooperated fully with Marino and decided to become more involved in preparation for his trial, including participation in jury selection.

"We can't choose anyone who laughs a lot, Mr. Marino," he said earnestly. "We have to stay away from the muscular type that act like they're the greatest and who like to make fun of everything." He paused, then added emphatically, "And no niggers. Just older people."

But as Oliver rambled, Marino's attention was not on the selection of a jury. He was thinking more about the upcoming pre-trial hearing which would determine whether Oliver's written and videotaped confessions could be admitted as evidence in the trial. Marino's strongest hope was to convince the judge that Oliver's confessions had not been given voluntarily and knowingly, and therefore they should not be permitted at the trial. He prepared to argue that since Oliver was tricked and emotionally coerced into the confessions, they should be thrown out.

The hearings began in February, in a Nassau County courtroom in Mineola, the county seat on Long Island. The presiding judge was Supreme Court

Justice John S. Thorp, Jr., who had been on the bench for thirteen years.

Throughout the hearings Oliver rarely displayed any emotion and often kept his head down on the table in front of him. His first visible reaction came when he was shown the twelve-minute videotape of his confession and burst into tears. But shortly afterward, his face again became expressionless and he resumed his slouched posture.

The only time Oliver's face brightened was when he saw Karlene enter the courtroom and walk toward the front row of spectator seats.

On the first day she wore the white jumpsuit he had bought for her at the mall, and Oliver noticed heads turning to stare at her beauty. Her hair had grown and flowed softly to her shoulders. Oliver's eyes filled with tears as he watched his Angel, who he thought looked like a movie star. Later, reading about the hearing in a local newspaper, he discovered that he was not alone; one reporter had called her a Robin Givens look-alike.

"Your honor," Marino was addressing the judge, "we are not dealing here with guilt or innocence, but the way the confession was obtained."

Oliver wasn't listening to his lawyer but was staring at Angel, who mouthed to him, "I love you."

He picked up a pen and started scribbling on a yellow legal pad that was lying on the table in front of him. When he had finished writing he held up the pad for Karlene to read his note. It said, "It's been four weeks. I haven't had one letter."

She mouthed back to him that she was looking for engagement rings.

Oliver, in turn, blew her kisses. Over the next few

hours he wrote several other notes to Karlene and held them up for her to read. "How did you get to court?" one note said. "Where are you staying?" he wrote on another.

Oliver read her lips as she mouthed back answers to his questions.

When he wrote, "Visit me today. Wait for me at the jail in case I'm back late," Karlene mouthed back that she was afraid to visit him in jail because the last time she had gone, three guards had tried to pick her up.

As the hearing progressed, Marino decided to call Karlene to the stand to testify on Oliver's behalf. But before the witness was called, Cotter intervened.

"I would indicate that, based upon the investigation of this case," he said, "I think it would be appropriate to advise Miss Francis of her constitutional rights against self-incrimination and the right to have counsel present, based on everything that I know of in this case."

When the judge asked for more specific details, Cotter proceeded to explain that a written and signed statement by Karlene indicated some involvement and knowledge prior to the homicides, involvement in lying to the police and disposing of physical evidence with Oliver.

Marino insisted that his questioning would not incriminate Karlene, but Cotter added that his own questions on cross-examination might subject her to criminal liability in the future.

When Karlene was finally duly sworn and took the stand as a witness, Judge Thorp spoke to her first.

"Your name is Karlene Francis?"

"Yes," she answered in a whisper.

"You have been sitting in the courtroom while this proceeding was going on?" the judge asked.

"Yes."

"You heard Mr. Cotter say that he had certain information about your activities during the time before and on the day of the incident which is the subject of this case."

"Yes."

"Did you understand that?" Judge Thorp asked.

"Yes," she answered meekly.

The judge proceeded. "I know from previous testimony that you were present in the home in Great Neck on or about the time of the incident which is the subject of this proceeding. Do you have an attorney?"

"No."

"Have you discussed the case with an attorney, in any way, other than Mr. Marino?"

"No."

"Do you have the funds to hire an attorney?"

"No."

"Are you aware of the fact that under the United States Constitution you have a privilege against self-incrimination?"

"Yes."

"Do you know what that means?"

"No, no," she answered, with tears welling up in her eyes.

Judge Thorp explained the privilege to Karlene and advised her to consult with an attorney before answering any questions. He then assigned Kenneth Shapiro, of the Office of the Legal Aid Society, to consult with her to determine how she should respond as a witness in the proceeding.

A lunch recess was taken to give Karlene an opportunity to confer with her new attorney, who advised her that it would not be in her best interests to testify and that if she were recalled to the witness stand she should assert her Fifth Amendment right as to incrimination.

Marino, however, renewed his request to recall her to the stand. He insisted that Karlene was a relevant material witness to the admissibility of statements that Oliver had made during the time he was in police custody. Shaking his head in anger, his voice rose as he argued that the D.A.'s threatening to prosecute Karlene for murder if she served as a witness for the defense was chilling, a deprivation of due process of law, and would deny his client a fair hearing and trial.

After extensive delays Judge Thorp called Karlene back to the witness stand, where she was reminded that she was still under oath. He asked her if she understood her constitutional privilege under the Fifth Amendment to the U.S. Constitution, and she answered softly, "Yes."

He asked her if she intended to exercise that right to all questions asked of her, and again she responded, "Yes."

As some of the questions were being read back by the court reporter, Karlene suddenly blurted out, "I will testify."

"I'm sorry?" the judge asked, as if he hadn't heard correctly.

"I will testify," she repeated.

"You will testify?" Judge Thorp asked.

Karlene nodded. "Yes."

After a brief conference between Karlene and her assigned lawyer, Shapiro approached the bench and said to the judge, "Your Honor, after consulting with my client, she has said she wants to testify. I want it to be clear that I advised her that it's not in her best interest, that she should assert her Fifth Amendment privilege. And that contrary to my advice, she has elected to testify."

Following a few minutes' delay for further clarification of several points, Marino took a deep breath and proceeded with his questioning of Karlene Francis.

In a voice that could barely be heard, Karlene answered questions about her interrogation, both outside of Oliver's house and at police headquarters, about her separation from Oliver and the refusal of police officers to allow her to see or speak to him. She described her conversations with Detective Milgrim and the detective's promise that if she told them what had really happened Oliver wouldn't go to jail but to a psychiatric hospital.

Obediently she recounted how she had been taken into Oliver's interrogation room and tried to persuade him to talk, how Oliver had warned her that it was a trick but she had reassured him that it would be okay.

Marino moved closer to Karlene as he asked gently, "Did you say this because you believed the police would live up to their word and send Oliver Petrovich to the psychiatric hospital instead of the jail?"

She answered softly, "Yes."

The following morning Dan Cotter began his cross-examination of Karlene Francis, with Kenneth Shapiro sitting nearby. As Cotter fired questions at Karlene about her conversations with Detective Milgrim and other events at issue, she answered timidly, "I will not answer that question on the basis that I'm exercising my Fifth Amendment privilege."

Cotter proceeded expertly and Karlene answered the majority of his questions with, "I don't remember," or, "I refuse to answer; I'm exercising my Fifth Amendment privilege."

Losing patience, Cotter finally approached Judge Thorp. "Judge," he said, "based on the witness's refusal to answer questions dealing directly—questions and conversations between herself and Detective Milgrim—I would at this time move to strike her direct testimony."

Marino looked angry and objected, asking the court to deny this motion. He accused Cotter of deliberately trying to create an impression that Karlene was an uncooperative witness.

But Cotter persisted, arguing that Karlene's refusal to answer was proof that she was not telling the truth about conversations with Detective Milgrim. Again he requested that Karlene's testimony be stricken.

Judge Thorp listened to the debate between the two attorneys, and then ruled with a denial of the application to strike the direct testimony of Karlene Francis.

On April 11 Marino called Dr. Alan Klein to the stand. After reviewing his background and credentials and establishing his specialty in forensic psychology, Marino offered Dr. Klein to the court as an expert in psychology.

Marino asked Klein about the tests he had selected for Oliver's psychological evaluation.

Dr. Klein answered that a comprehensive psychological evaluation should consider different aspects of an individual's functioning. He explained why he had chosen the particular tests, and under Marino's direction he proceeded to describe the format of each and the conclusions he had arrived at after his evaluation.

"In administering the Wechsler Adult Intelligence Scale to Mr. Petrovich, I find that there is an extreme disparity between the verbal and nonverbal scales," Dr. Klein explained. "Extreme to the extent that differences in scores as large as the ones that have been obtained are highly unlikely to have occurred simply by chance and would indicate some particular deficits. Mr. Petrovich has obtained a verbal IQ score of 79. This particular score would place him at the eighth percentile in the general population. In other words, approximately 92 percent of all individuals would obtain scores equal to or higher than his score of 79.

"On the other hand, he's obtained a performance IQ score of 112, which would then be equal to the 79th percentile of the general population, or that approximately 21 percent of all individuals would have scores equal to or higher than that.

"The difference in IQ score points of 33 is considered to be a highly significant difference and indicative of a wide disparity in intellectual functioning."

"Dr. Klein," Marino asked, "would you classify the verbal IQ score of Oliver Petrovich as being borderline retarded?"

"It would be within that general area, yes," he answered.

After further questions to Dr. Klein about his test observations of Oliver's overall thinking, functioning, and stress tolerance, Marino asked, "Now Dr. Klein, taking into consideration all that you have testified about up to now, do you have an opinion as to whether or not, with a reasonable degree of psychological certainty, Oliver Petrovich, on September 25, 1988, was capable of understanding and appreciating the nature and consequences of his waiver of his constitutional rights, commonly known as the Miranda warnings?"

"It is my opinion that his appreciation of his waiver of his Miranda rights would have been extremely limited," he answered.

When Marino asked Dr. Klein what it might mean that Oliver broke down and cried upon seeing himself on videotape, Dr. Klein replied that Oliver's response indicated that the experience had a severe emotional impact, and certainly not the one that would have been anticipated.

Marino's questions then turned to Karlene and the relationship between Oliver and Karlene, which Dr. Klein described as obsessional in nature.

Marino asked him, "Based on your understanding and opinion as to this relationship as it existed back on September 25, 1988, what is your opinion with respect to whether or not Oliver Petrovich would do whatever Karlene Francis asked him to do?"

Once again, Dr. Klein answered thoughtfully and professionally. "Perhaps I can clarify this most if I were to use an analogy. The analogy would be one of an individual who is alone at sea and comes across a piece of floating wood. That individual becomes extremely attached to that piece of floating wood, almost as a means of life survival. The relationship between Oliver Petrovich and Karlene Francis carries elements of that kind of clinging."

When Marino asked Dr. Klein what effect Karlene's presence in Oliver's interrogation room would have had on Oliver, the witness replied, "I think that would certainly have a great impact on Oliver Petrovich. That confrontation would have the result of breaking the dam that was holding back all of his feelings. I think he was put in a position unable to resist, responding regardless of what he may have perceived as his own best interests."

"Now, Doctor," Marino concluded, "do you have an opinion as to whether or not Oliver Petrovich would have answered police questions but for the confrontation and information from Karlene Francis?"

With authority Alan Klein answered, "My opinion is that he would not have spoken to the police."

In Cotter's cross-examination of Dr. Klein he tried to discredit the psychological evaluations of Oliver Petrovich and to suggest that Oliver had been calculating while taking the tests and had manipulated his responses to suit his best interests.

When Cotter asked Dr. Klein if Oliver's motivation to discredit the statements he had given might have affected his test performance, the witness conceded that it was a consideration.

The possibility of Oliver intentionally scoring lower on his tests was the subject of questioning, but Dr. Klein insisted that in his professional opinion, this was not the case.

Cotter then directed his questions toward Oliver's ability to understand his Miranda rights.

"Doctor," he asked the witness. "Are you aware that the defendant wanted to be a police officer?"

"Yes," Dr. Klein replied.

"Is it your testimony, Doctor," Cotter pushed, "that this individual who has had this interest in police work, who had seen it on television numerous times and has been a defendant in prior criminal proceedings doesn't understand that when a detective says, 'You have the right to remain silent,' that means, 'You don't have to talk to me'?"

But Dr. Klein remained firm that Oliver's interest in police work and personal involvement did not guarantee his ability to succeed as a police officer or his understanding of his rights.

Cotter's mind was racing. He was aware that Oliver had written several letters to Marino, and that these letters had been among the materials used by Dr. Klein in completing his psychological evaluation. But the letters had not been included in the file given to Cotter. Up to this minute he hadn't been certain whether he would need them for evidence, but now he decided that they were vital to his case, and asked Judge Thorp to be provided with them.

Marino, angered by this suggestion, refused to turn over the letters, emphasizing to the judge that they were attorney/client-privileged and confidential letters, mailed directly to Nicholas Marino at his office from Oliver Petrovich at the Nassau County Jail.

But Cotter would not back down. "I submit that these letters are directly relevant to the issues of understanding and comprehension of something as basic as the Miranda warnings."

With heightened emotions they continued to debate the issue of Oliver's letters and their relevance in Klein's evaluation.

Marino was unwilling to relent and finally asked for an adjournment in order to research the legal issue of privilege. "We're not talking about a small issue here," he said. "We're talking about a tremendously important issue with regard to attorney/client privilege."

Judge Thorp granted his request for an adjournment of one week. Following the adjournment, Marino presented the court with several hours' worth of research and past cases to substantiate his point that Oliver's letters were privileged material. After further debate between the two lawyers, Judge Thorp ruled that delivering the letters would be a constitutional violation and that they would remain privileged and confidential.

The pre-trial hearing continued until June 1, when final arguments were presented.

On July 12 Judge Thorp released his twelve-page decision. He found the testimony of each of the witnesses to be credible, except for that of Karlene Francis, which he ruled lacked credibility.

He also found that the defendant was not in custody prior to the time that Detective Parpan advised him of his constitutional Miranda rights at approximately 10:30 A.M. on September 25, 1988, and accordingly statements made prior to that time would not be suppressed.

The court further found that Detective Parpan properly advised the defendant of his constitutional rights, and the defendant acknowledged that he understood them and thereupon knowingly, intelligently, and voluntarily waived his rights before making his statements to the police.

"This defendant," Judge Thorp wrote, "clearly had the ability to understand the immediate meaning of the waiver, and thus his waiver was valid.

"Even with the assumption that confronting the defendant with Francis contributed to the defendant's ultimate decision to make inculpatory admissions, it does not render them involuntarily made," the judge ruled, adding, "it is not improper for the police to confront the defendant with evidence which they believe to be inconsistent with what he has told them."

Judge Thorp ruled that there was no credible evidence that the police themselves, or through Francis, induced the defendant to make a statement by promising him that he would be hospitalized rather than incarcerated, and accordingly the oral statements made to Parpan and Donnelly and the written statement taken by Parpan would not be suppressed.

The videotaped statement taken later that evening likewise would not be suppressed. Judge Thorp wrote: "It is notable that in giving the videotaped statement, the defendant does not merely give monosyllabic responses to leading questions but rather speaks in narrative form about the events of the night in question, thus further evidencing his intellectual ability to comprehend his constitutional rights."

When Marino heard Judge Thorp's decision his face dropped. "We're disappointed at the ruling," he admitted, "but we're prepared to go to trial."

Chapter 18:
AUGUST 1988
"MAY I SEE SOME ID?"

"Police Officer Oliver Petrovich, report to duty."

A sudden banging noise startled Oliver, and he jumped. As his eyes flew open he realized with the familiar sinking feeling that he was not in a police uniform at headquarters, but in a prison uniform at the Nassau County Jail.

Since the recent hearings Oliver had spent many hours thinking about what it would have been like to pass the police test and become an officer. Now he would never know the feeling of belonging that he had dreamed of so often.

Many nights Oliver had studied the police manual, with Angel cuddled next to him, and he had even gone to several recruitment meetings that the New York Police Department held at different public high schools. He knew he needed a high school diploma or equivalency to become a cop, but he told himself he'd worry about that after he passed the police test. Oliver had bought his used police cruiser to get ready for being a real cop. Driving up and down the highway, he had pretended and practiced being a police officer. To Oliver, that was the best part. When other drivers saw his car and automatically slowed down, he felt a surge of power. He knew that his car, painted black, looked exactly like an unmarked police car. But to make it even more convincing, Oliver had gone to an auto parts store to buy a flashing red light.

At first the store owner had looked at him suspiciously. "Anyone in your family a cop?" he had asked.

"Yeah, my uncle," Oliver had answered without looking at him.

He must have been convincing enough, because the man had sold him the light. Oliver had hooked it up to his car and when he plugged it in and put it on the roof of his car, it rotated and made his cruiser look even more like the real thing.

With a new burst of confidence Oliver waited for the next evening when Angel was visiting her sister. He put on a pair of dark slacks and matching shirt, pinned a phony badge to his shirt and took his car out to the Meadowbrook Parkway. Driving along the parkway, Oliver studied the other cars passing by and peered inside to check out the drivers and passengers, waiting for the first opportunity to test his authority.

When he saw a young male driver in a black

Porsche speeding southbound on the parkway, Oliver decided to make his move. He turned on his light and accelerated to catch up to the Porsche, signaling the driver to pull over.

When the Porsche came to a stop on the shoulder Oliver pulled in front of him, got out of his cruiser and walked confidently over to the other car.

"May I see some ID?" he asked, in a serious tone.

"Officer," the young man answered urgently, "I'm an off-duty police officer." He showed Oliver his badge. "I know I was speeding, but I'm late for a wedding." He looked at Oliver as if to say, "Come on, you understand, don't you?"

As Oliver realized that he had just pulled over a real cop, he began to feel a horrible sense of panic rising within him, praying that it was too dark for this officer to see that he wasn't wearing a uniform, and that his badge was fake. Desperately he tried to stay cool.

"Okay, take it easy," he answered the young officer in the Porsche. "Have fun at the wedding."

"Hey, thanks a lot." The off-duty officer stuck out his hand to shake Oliver's and started his car.

Oliver walked slowly back to his own car, only wishing that Angel could have been there to witness the scene, because he knew she'd never believe him.

When Oliver had first told his parents that he wanted to be a cop, his mother had understood his dreams but discouraged them because she was frightened of her son having such a dangerous job.

"You'll get hurt, Olly. It's too dangerous," she had repeated again and again, trying to persuade him to change his mind.

But when Oliver told his father about his plans, his

response was one of anger. When his father had finished yelling at Oliver and calling him stupid, he
started to laugh, which made Oliver feel even worse
that his father didn't take him seriously.

Over the next few months, every time Oliver mentioned his plans for studying to be a police officer, his
father would just look at him and laugh. He was hu-
miliated by his father, and equally frustrated by his
mother, who sat there passively and listened to his
father, not even trying to defend him.

After twenty-three years, Oliver finally gave up hope
that there was anything he could ever do to make his
parents understand him.

Chapter 19:
SEPTEMBER 25–28, 1989
"YOU MUST KEEP AN OPEN MIND"

"People versus Oliver Petrovich," announced the court clerk. "Indictment 69495. For trial. Are the People ready?"

"People are ready, Judge," answered Dan Cotter.

"Defendant ready?" asked the clerk.

"The defendant is ready," responded Nick Marino.

"Both sides are ready," announced the clerk.

For the first time Judge John Thorp spoke. "Good

morning, ladies and gentlemen," he addressed the group of prospective jurors. "My name is Judge Thorp. I'm the judge who will be presiding at this trial concerning which you have been called over to this courtroom from the Central Jury Room as prospective jurors."

Judge Thorp explained to the prospective jurors what their role would be during the trial and briefly described the case of "The People of the State of New York against Oliver Petrovich." He pointed out the defendant and both the defense and prosecuting attorneys. Finally he explained the process by which the trial would be conducted and by which they would come to a final verdict.

The judge emphasized, "Only you, as members of the trial jury, can determine guilt, and the defendant is presumed innocent unless and until you do find him guilty."

After Judge Thorp advised the group that the trial was expected to last approximately two weeks, the process of selecting a jury began. General questions were put to the group by the judge, followed by questions from both Marino and Cotter. Each prospective juror was then called individually to the bench for an interview.

Finally fourteen names were read, and those individuals were instructed to take seats in the jury box before recessing for lunch.

When they reconvened at 2:15, Judge Thorp continued to question the fourteen prospective jurors and explained to the group the basic principles of law involved in the case.

"The defendant is presumed to be innocent," he stressed again. "He is not required to prove anything.

The entire burden of proof in this case, as in every criminal case, rests with the People. A defendant is presumed to be innocent until his guilt has been established to the satisfaction of a jury beyond a reasonable doubt."

Before dismissing the group for the final selection, Judge Thorp reminded them that the function of the jury selection process was to find twelve jurors who could keep an open mind until they heard the entire case, and only then, listening to the views of the other eleven jurors and by reasoning and deliberating together, arrive at a unanimous verdict.

On September 27 at 4:15 P.M. a jury of twelve and two alternates were sworn in by the clerk of the court. Of the fourteen selected, there were seven men and seven women. All were Caucasian except for one Oriental man. Eight of the jurors were parents themselves, three were single, and three married but with no children. Of those three, one woman was pregnant with her first child.

After Judge Thorp reviewed instructions and reminded the jury of the rules of conduct for the trial, he adjourned the court until the following morning, when opening statements would begin.

When Dan Cotter addressed a jury, he had their undivided attention. In the tiny Mineola courtroom he knew how to use his size, voice, and subtle drama to his advantage. Although he rarely lost his cool, when Cotter became impassioned, his upper lip began to perspire. The jury might have missed this subtlety or might not have noticed his conservative gray suit, but they would not forget his powerful presentation of each point during the three-week trial.

Since the indictment a year ago Cotter had devoted a day or two each week to preparing for the trial. At the same time he maintained his regular caseload of about twenty cases in various stages. The most highly publicized of the cases Cotter was prosecuting was that of Robert Golub, a twenty-two-year-old Long Island man accused of murdering and dismembering Kelly Tinyes, his thirteen-year-old neighbor. In late September the Golub case was in the midst of pre-trial hearings, and Cotter, while arduously preparing his case, was simultaneously working on his opening statement for the prosecution of Oliver Petrovich.

"If it pleases the Court, Judge Thorp, Mr. Marino, ladies and gentlemen of the jury," he began, "it's my opportunity now to give you a little preview of what I expect to be some of the testimony, some of the exhibits that will be produced at this trial, and to lay out for you, if you will, how I intend to prove that the defendant committed the two counts contained in the indictment against him."

Cotter went on to explain that it was the People's burden to show that Oliver intended to cause the deaths of his parents and that he succeeded.

Cotter walked toward the jury box as he continued to talk to the twelve jurors. He vowed to them that during the trial he would produce proof that Oliver Petrovich not only intentionally killed his parents, but intended to conceal the crimes. He vowed to prove that Oliver had been plotting for months to kill his father, that his hate for his father had been simmering within him for a long time and that the murder was planned and calculated.

"The defendant is a twenty-three-year-old young man," Cotter continued. "This is not an infant or a juvenile. He held a job taking home almost four hundred dollars a week. Why didn't he choose to go to Las Vegas, get married, start a life somewhere else with Karlene Francis? He chose instead to plan the murder of his parents, to inherit his parents' home and their twenty-unit apartment building in Queens, worth in the neighborhood of one million dollars."

As Cotter continued to discuss the testimony the jury would hear during the trial, he advised them to listen carefully and critically to each witness. "You'll not find any crazy defendant," he said firmly.

Looking from one face to the next, he added, "So while you know it's shocking that a son could turn on his father whom he might not like, could turn on his mother, the person that gave birth to him and brought him into this world, all to inherit their monetary assets, it happens."

When explaining that they would be viewing Oliver's videotaped confession, Cotter advised the jury to listen to Oliver's tone and lack of remorse.

"Listen to the planning and premeditation," he said. "You will hear how the defendant tells what happened in a narrative. 'I went in, I shot him once, then I shot him again,' Oliver said. And when the district attorney asked him what happened next, he replied, 'Then he was dead.' As calmly as that."

Before concluding his opening remarks, Cotter warned the jury against accepting opinions from witnesses who offered themselves as experts without listening very carefully to all of the facts.

"And I submit to you," he finished, "that the People will have proved beyond a reasonable doubt that on the evening of September 24 and the morning of September 25, 1988, the defendant intentionally killed both his mother and his father."

After thanking the jury and returning to his seat, Cotter looked toward the judge, who said, "Mr. Marino, you may proceed."

Nick Marino always used his hands while speaking to a jury, and often paced back and forth. "It's the Italian in me," he would explain lightly to anyone who commented on his animated gestures.

Since his first meeting with Oliver, Marino had continued to visit him regularly at the Nassau County Jail and as the date for the trial approached he had spent increasingly more time working on Oliver's defense. His greatest hope for the case lay in the psychiatric and psychological evidence, which he reviewed over and over again. He also read and reread the transcripts from the pre-trial hearings, hoping to find inconsistencies in the testimonies of Detectives Parpan and Donnelly, and trying to anticipate how they would testify during the trial. On the morning of September 28 Marino was ready with his opening statement.

After greeting the jury, Marino began by emphasizing how important it was for the jurors to keep an open mind in order to give Oliver Petrovich the opportunity for a fair trial.

As he spoke to the individual jurors, he walked back and forth in front of the jury box, trying to create a picture of Oliver that would generate the sympathy he needed.

"You are going to hear a sad story about a twenty-three-year-old young man living in his mother and father's house and treated like a stranger," Marino told the jury. "This young man was not treated like a son, but like a person who lived in a guest room."

Marino recounted the series of events from Oliver's first meeting Karlene up to the night of September 24.

"The pressures built, the tension built, factors were developing over a period of months. There was a simmering within his mind, and then the explosion occurred."

As Marino's voice filled with emotion, he introduced the side of Oliver unable to deal with stress, unable to reason intelligently.

"You've got to focus on this state of mind that existed at the time in question, when Oliver Petrovich was extremely disturbed and did not have the ability to choose between his parents and their rules, to pick between Karlene or Mom and Dad."

Insisting that Oliver did not appreciate the nature and consequences of his actions, Marino concluded, "And that's what this case is all about, ladies and gentlemen. You have to decide this case on whether or not Oliver Petrovich acted reasonably given the extreme emotions that he was under at the time. I submit to you that Oliver Petrovich was not a man who was able to make choices freely, without assistance from others."

After asking the jury once again to keep an open mind in the case, Marino thanked them and returned to his seat next to Oliver.

Judge Thorp addressed the court. "Thank you, gentlemen. Mr. Cotter, will you please call the first witness?"

The first two witnesses for the People were Police Officer Frank Tappan of the sixth precinct, who was covering the Great Neck area in his patrol car on September 28, and was the first to arrive at the Petrovich house in Great Neck on the night of the murder, and Michael Wiley, the medical examiner who examined the victims at the scene. Each witness was questioned by Cotter, cross-examined by Marino, re-questioned by Cotter, and finally re-cross-examined by Marino.

When the court called for the next witness, Cotter knew how important his testimony would be. As he stood and glanced over at the jury, Cotter announced the name of Vincent Wilson as a witness on behalf of the People.

Chapter 20:
MAY–AUGUST 1988
"THERE'S JUST NO WAY OUT"

"Hey, Vinnie, you've got to help me," Oliver pleaded to his co-worker at the Pepsi plant. "I've really got trouble."

"What gives, Petrovich?" the big black man asked as they cleaned themselves off after working under a greasy truck.

"I need a gun." Oliver was speaking softly but there was an urgency in his voice that convinced Vincent Wilson that this was no joke.

The two men had been working together as truck mechanics for a little over a year, and although they never socialized after hours, they often fooled around together on the job and sometimes got into trouble racing trucks in the yard or goofing off when they were supposed to be working. Wilson liked to have a good time with Oliver, but he took his job seriously and recently had started to avoid Oliver because hanging out with him meant trouble.

Just the week before, Wilson had gotten a warning letter from his supervisor after Oliver had persuaded him to spray some of the other workers with their high-pressure hoses. When Oliver saw Wilson's letter he started to laugh and continued laughing until Wilson finally snapped at him, "I don't want to be involved in your shit, Petrovich." Shortly afterward, when Oliver received his own warning letter for poor behavior on the job, he found nothing funny about it and sulked for the next few days.

Now, looking at Oliver's face, Wilson sensed that whatever was on his mind, it was serious.

"Hey, man, what are you talking about?" Wilson looked at Oliver with curious concern.

"Vinnie, I can't take it anymore. Can you get me a gun with a silencer?"

Wilson stopped rubbing the grease off his arm and stared at Oliver. "Why?" he asked.

"I want to kill my father," Oliver answered calmly. "He keeps harassing me and Angel."

Wilson already knew all about Angel. Oliver had told him about her shortly after they had first met, and he knew how much Oliver was in love with his Angel. He also knew that she had secretly moved in with him and that Oliver's father hated her because she was black.

Wilson had met Angel several times when she had

come to the Pepsi plant and waited for Oliver to get off from work at the end of the day. They had only had a few brief conversations, but Wilson was impressed by the change that came over Oliver the moment he saw his Angel.

He looked into Oliver's eyes and put his large hand on Oliver's arm. "I don't know where to get a gun, Petrovich," he said. "And that's a crazy idea." He took his hand back and looked away. "Hey, why don't you look for a furnished room somewhere for you and Angel?"

Oliver smiled at the suggestion. "Yeah, that's a good idea," he answered as he picked up a tool to return to work on the truck.

Three months passed and Wilson heard no more from Oliver about needing a gun. He dismissed it from his mind, hoping that it was just another crazy whim of his impulsive co-worker.

Oliver fooled around less at work and kept more to himself. When he and Wilson were working near each other, Oliver occasionally talked about Angel and some of the things they did together. As finishing time grew closer, Wilson noticed enviously that Oliver kept glancing over at the clock and seemed fidgety, as if he couldn't wait to get out of there and to his Angel.

One morning in August while Wilson and Oliver were working together repairing one of the Pepsi trucks, sweating from the heat of the summer day, Oliver again brought up Angel and the trouble he was having at home. "My mom knows she's staying at the house," he confided to Wilson, "but my father has no idea. He'd definitely throw me out of the house if he knew. He's going to be on a two-week vacation at the end of September and he'll be home all the time. I don't know what we'll do then." Oliver turned to look at Wilson. "Do you think you could put Angel up in your apartment?"

"I'd like to help you out, Petrovich, but I'm married. I've got a wife at home; I can't put Angel up in my apartment." Wilson saw the worried expression on Oliver's face. "Why don't you pick up the *Amsterdam News* where they advertise rented rooms?" he suggested. "I bet you can find a cheap room."

"Okay, that's a good idea," Oliver answered hopefully.

During his lunch break Oliver bought a newspaper and the two men looked through it together. When Wilson pointed out a room in Jamaica, Queens, advertised for fifty-five dollars a month, he circled it in the newspaper for Oliver and encouraged him to call the number listed.

"Yeah, okay, sounds good," Oliver agreed as he folded the paper and put it in his pocket. But Oliver knew that he would never do it. With Angel not working and depending on him for everything, he could never afford to pay the rent and other expenses that would come with an apartment. If he had to pay for an apartment, he'd never be able to make the payments on his car insurance.

While walking slowly back toward the truck to finish his assigned repairs, Oliver was thinking to himself, "There's just no way out."

Chapter 21: SEPTEMBER 28–OCTOBER 11, 1989

"I WAS TEMPORARILY INSANE"

"Mr. Wilson, where do you currently work?" Cotter asked the witness.

"Pepsi-Cola Bottling Company," he answered softly, looking straight ahead, never turning toward Oliver.

"What do you do for Pepsi-Cola?"

"I'm a mechanic."

"And did Oliver Petrovich work with you at Pepsi-Cola?"

"Yes."

"What job did he have?" Cotter continued.

"Mechanical helper," Wilson responded.

Several questions later Cotter asked Wilson, "Mr. Wilson, did there come a time in May of 1988 that you ever had a conversation with this defendant about a gun?"

"Yes," he answered, still reluctant to make any eye contact.

"What type of gun did he ask for?"

"A gun with a silencer."

"Did he say what he wanted that gun for?"

"To kill his father."

Vincent Wilson testified that Oliver had asked him to let Karlene live with him while Oliver's father took his vacation, that he had told Oliver he had nowhere to put her and had suggested he get a newspaper and look for an apartment.

In cross-examination Marino directed his questioning toward Wilson's awareness of Oliver's fear of his father and of his concern for Karlene.

"Did Oliver express to you great concern for Angel, his girlfriend?" he asked the witness.

"Well, he told me that he loved her," he answered, sneaking a glance at Oliver.

"And did he tell you that he was afraid of his father?"

"Yes, he said that if his father found Angel in the house, he would throw him out."

"Did he ever indicate to you that he wanted to kill his mother?"

"No, he didn't say that."

* * *

During the testimony of Vincent Wilson, Oliver sat listlessly in his seat, staring down at the table in front of him. He wore a simple navy blue suit his cousin Terry had bought for him for his trial, with a plain white shirt and nondescript tie. Never having had an interest in fashion, Oliver didn't care that his brown shoes didn't match the one suit that he wore every day of the trial.

His cousin Terry was the only one from Oliver's family who came to the trial. All his other relatives from both sides of the family had refused to have anything to do with him since the night his parents died. To them, Oliver was also dead.

While he listened to the witnesses being questioned, Oliver occasionally shredded a napkin on the table in front of him, but his face showed no emotion and it was impossible for anyone watching him to tell what was going on inside his mind.

After Wilson had stepped down from the witness chair, Oliver listened with the same emptiness to testimony by other police officers and members of the Crime Scene Search Unit. He watched photographs of his house and of his parents' bodies being submitted as evidence. He heard Marino object to the use of several of the more gruesome photos, especially the close-up shots of his father that focused on his gunshot wounds. Marino insisted that they were inflammatory, and would have no purpose but to inflame the jury and prejudice them against his client. But Cotter argued for the use of the photos, in that they depicted evidence relevant and material to the case. Finally the judge allowed two of the photos to be used as evidence, and dismissed two others. Throughout the debate Oliver sat passively and stared at the napkin he had finished shredding. Nobody in the courtroom saw any emotion from him, until the moment he learned that Karlene would not be testifying on his behalf at his trial.

Oliver's defense received a severe blow that afternoon in the judge's chambers, when Marino was informed that Peggy Forman of the Nassau County Legal Aid Society had been appointed as counsel to Karlene, and that on her advice Karlene had decided not to testify at the trial.

"I have spoken to Miss Francis," Forman said, "and she has indicated to me that, if she is called as a witness by the defense, she will take the Fifth Amendment in response to any questions asked of her."

As Marino listened to this unexpected news, and a following request by Forman that he not speak to Karlene anymore without her being present, he fought to control his anger.

He argued that Karlene had indicated that she wished to testify on behalf of Oliver, and that in view of that decision, it was important for him to meet with her to discuss what she was planning to say. He insisted that by prohibiting him from meeting alone with Karlene, the court would be putting him at a great disadvantage and prejudicing his case.

After listening patiently to Marino, Judge Thorp responded that he felt Karlene Francis was in need of legal assistance and legal representation before she would appear in any further proceeding in the case. He also approved Forman's request that she be present in any interviews between Karlene and Marino.

Marino knew that Karlene's testimony was critical to Oliver's defense. She was the only person who could testify from personal knowledge about the relationship between Oliver and his parents.

He tried to reason with the judge. "For me to be unable to explore these important issues with the only other person alive in the world, other than Oliver Petrovich, who knows what went on in that home, is in essence to deny my client effective assistance of counsel, and ultimately is to deny him a fair trial here."

Judge Thorp answered Marino, "Well, of course until the witness is actually called, and with her own mouth announces her position, we can't know what she will do. In fact, she changed her mind at the pre-trial hearing."

Several days later, when Marino announced that he would call Karlene Francis for his first witness for the defense, Cotter expressed to the Court his reservations over her history of changing her mind when sitting on the stand, and his concern that she would continue to invoke the Fifth Amendment privilege, as she had during the pre-trial hearing.

Judge Thorp, after listening to both lawyers, decided to bring Karlene into the courtroom without the presence of the jury, and to make a determination as to how she intended to proceed.

After Karlene was sworn in, Judge Thorp asked Peggy Forman, who had accompanied Karlene, if she had any statement to make.

Forman repeated for the record that she had informed Mr. Marino and the Court that Karlene did not intend to testify and would exercise her Fifth Amendment privilege.

The judge turned to Karlene. "Have you discussed

this prospective testimony with Miss Forman, the attorney I appointed to represent you?"

"Yes," she answered in a whisper.

"Has she advised you as to the implications of possible self-incrimination?" he asked her.

"Yes."

"Has she advised you that you have a privilege, under the Fifth Amendment of the United States Constitution, not to testify?" Judge Thorp continued.

Karlene nodded her head up and down.

"Yes or no?" the judge persisted.

"Yes," she answered meekly.

"Have you made a decision as to how you intend to proceed?"

"Yes."

"What do you intend to do?"

"To exercise the Fifth Amendment," Karlene answered.

"Is it your intention that you would exercise your Fifth Amendment rights of all questions asked by Mr. Marino or Mr. Cotter?"

"Yes," she repeated softly.

"Thank you," Judge Thorp said to her. "You may step down." As Karlene was excused, a disappointed Marino watched his most important witness leave the courtroom.

He requested that the jury be told that Karlene had been called by the Defense to testify and that, due to legal reasons, she would not be testifying. But Judge Thorp rejected his request.

About thirty minutes later, as the court was ready to adjourn for the day and Judge Thorp was in the middle of dismissing the jury, Oliver, with no warning, suddenly blurted out, "My girlfriend was here." He pointed to the judge and continued. "He said she could testify without the jury, but she can't testify in front of the jury. Mr. Cotter has a 97 percent conviction rate. He is allowed to get five cops to testify in front of the jury—"

Judge Thorp stopped Oliver with a stern voice. "Ladies and gentlemen, please disregard that outburst."

But Oliver was not finished. "I just got one witness. Cotter has five witnesses!"

"Ladies and gentlemen," Judge Thorp's voice was rising. "Please step into the jury room." While he spoke, two court officers sprang to posts beside Oliver.

As the twelve men and women of the jury started to get up to leave, Oliver was still shouting. "She doesn't come here, she comes here with an assistant D.A.! I got one witness only! She has to get thrown out! She is allowed to testify without the jury, but not in front of the jury!"

Amid loud confusion the jury was ushered out of the courtroom, and once again Oliver became emotionless.

Marino approached the judge. "Judge, for whatever it's worth," he said, "I apologize to the court for the outburst."

"That's not sufficient, Mr. Marino," Judge Thorp answered sternly. "I have to avoid a repetition of this."

Marino humbly apologized again, but Judge Thorp was not satisfied. "I have to take steps to make certain we do not have a repetition of that outburst," he said. Looking at Marino he added, "Now you have to talk to your client."

"I will," Marino answered.

"Right now." Judge Thorp was obviously angry.

"And give me an assurance that there will not be a repetition of that."

For the first time since his outburst, Oliver spoke. "Sorry, Judge. I was temporarily insane."

"Yes, I'm sure you were," the judge replied sarcastically, as the court clerk handed him a piece of paper that had been torn from a legal pad. Judge Thorp read the note quickly, then again addressed Marino. "Mr. Marino, I would also like to bring to your attention that the Court Clerk has just handed me a paper which was taken from the defendant during the course of the testimony of this witness, where there is printed in large block letters the following, meant for the jury to see: 'Thorp denied my girlfriend to testify in front of you.' I'm going to mark that as a court exhibit." He paused for an instant, looked again at Oliver, then continued, "Now I think it's fair to say, Mr. Marino, I have done my very best to give this defendant a fair trial and I have to knowingly make my own observation at this point, that the outburst by the defendant at that particular time was a very educated outburst. I am not going to permit any further outbursts by the defendant in this courtroom. If, in fact, that occurs again, then I will have to take steps to have him removed from the courtroom and make suitable arrangements for him to hear the balance of the proceedings from another room."

Following judge's warnings, the court was adjourned until the next morning.

Nick Marino was worried that the case for the defense was losing ground. Cotter's witnesses, one after another, had strengthened the People's case. A police officer from the Nassau County Marine Bureau had testified that he had retrieved the shotgun, with a spent cartridge still in the ejection port, in 15 feet of water off the Throgs Neck Bridge. Detective Donnelly had described the events of the evening of September 24, 1988, from the interrogation outside the Petrovich house and at police headquarters, to Oliver and Karlene being interviewed separately, being brought together, and finally confessing. Detective Parpan had also answered Cotter's questions about the interrogation and the confessions, and had agreed with Donnelly that there were no problems communicating with Oliver.

As Cotter had planned, the courtroom drama reached its climax when he asked Detective Parpan to read to the jury the written statement taken from Oliver on September 25, 1988. On cue, the witness had read slowly from the paper in front of him.

"I am Oliver Petrovich and I am 23 years old, having been born on January 8, 1965. I live at 64 Richard Avenue, Great Neck, with my parents and my girlfriend Angel stays there. I am currently employed by Pepsi-Cola as a mechanic helper in Mount Vernon.

"I have been told by Detective Parpan that I have the right to remain silent and that any statements I make may be used against me in court. I have been told that I have the right to talk with a lawyer before answering any questions, or to have a lawyer present at any time. Further, I have been advised that if I cannot afford to have a lawyer, one will be provided me, and I have the right to remain silent until I have had the chance to talk with a lawyer. I understand my rights and make the following statement freely and voluntarily."

Detective Parpan read Oliver's account of how he had first met Karlene at the shopping mall in New Rochelle and how he had nicknamed her Angel. Oliver mentioned that Karlene was having trouble with her landlady, and they had decided that she should move in with him. He described how he used to sneak her into the house and upstairs into his bedroom, how he told his mother and asked her not to tell his father, and she agreed. He told of how Karlene and his mother appeared to be getting along well, and everything was going smoothly until July, when his mother started to give him a hard time. He said that he was thinking about getting an apartment but realized that he couldn't afford one, and then, he admitted, he first thought about killing his parents.

The detective continued reading Oliver's statement. "Sometime around August I told Angel that I was thinking of killing my parents, so we wouldn't have to sneak around anymore. At first she said I was crazy, but as time went on and things were getting worse at home, she started to agree with me. She was never really convinced we should, but we did discuss it many times."

Oliver's statement then turned to Saturday, September 24, 1988, and he recounted the events of the day, starting with the building superintendent and his wife being invited over with another couple who had a nineteen-year-old daughter. He told of sneaking Angel out of the house and sending her to visit her sister, of his plan to get her back into the house, of his mother telling his father about Angel living there for all those months, and of his father yelling.

"During this yelling I started thinking again about killing my parents," Oliver said.

His statement was followed step-by-step with how he took his father's shotgun, practiced aiming it upstairs in his bedroom, walked through the house moving the gun from one place to another as he tried to figure out what to do.

"About this time Angel got to the house. It was about 11 P.M. I had been checking the window constantly for the past hour. My father had just gone to bed, and my mother was in the kitchen. I lifted Angel up through the window and snuck her upstairs. I stayed there with her about twenty minutes and told her I was ready to kill my parents. She didn't know what to do. Sometimes she was saying no, and other times she was trying to help me set up a cover-up for the cops. I told her to get into the closet and I came back downstairs. Just as I came down, my mother went into the bathroom. I used this time to move the gun from the dining room and put it under the kitchen table. I then sat down in the kitchen. My mother reentered the kitchen and I started talking with her. Before I could do anything, she left the kitchen and put the bird into its cage. She then came back into the kitchen. We were face-to-face talking and when she turned to go out, I decided to try to strangle her. I put my right arm around her throat and squeezed, trying to strangle her. She fought back and we both fell to the ground. I wanted to strangle her because it would have been quiet and I didn't want my father awake.

"When we fell to the ground, I let go of her throat and she started screaming. That's when I reached for the shotgun, which was right next to me. She was screaming and trying to get off the floor, trying to stand up. I was already up, and as she was getting up I aimed at the back of her head from point-blank, and shot her. She fell to the ground next to the wall, face down. I saw a lot of blood.

"Just about this time I heard my father and he was yelling. I immediately ran toward my father. When I got to the living room, I saw my father entering his bedroom. I fired once and believe I hit him on his side or his chest. The reason I hit his side was that in his room he was turning to look behind the door for the shotgun. After I hit him the first time, he went to the ground behind his bedroom door. I pulled the door away and aimed the gun at the right side of his head at point-blank range and fired. I knew that shot killed him."

The last part of Oliver's statement described what he and Karlene did afterward—how they decided to leave the house, get rid of the gun, and pretend that they hadn't been home when the shootings occurred. Oliver told of dropping the gun out the bathroom window, taking it with them in his father's car, throwing the gun off the Throgs Neck Bridge, and heading into Manhattan. Finally he told of returning home, calling his neighbor and telling the police the story that they had planned.

"I am presently at Nassau County, Homicide Squad, and I'm giving this statement to Detective Parpan and he is writing it for me. I have read this statement and it is the truth."

As soon as Detective Parpan had completed reading Oliver's statement, Judge Thorp cleared his throat. "Mr. Cotter?" he asked, waiting to see how the prosecutor planned to proceed.

"I have no further questions, Judge," he replied.

* * *

At the conclusion of the People's case, Marino moved to dismiss the indictment against Oliver Petrovich, for failure of the People to establish a *prima facie* case. "There are no witnesses to this crime," he said as he paced between the defense table and the jury box. "Other than the testimony or the alleged statements of my client, there is not direct evidence that my client committed this crime." Turning to the judge he continued, "I respectfully submit that the statements were taken in violation of my client's constitutional rights, and accordingly should be given no weight, and as a result, Your Honor, I respectfully move to dismiss this indictment against my client."

Judge Thorp responded without hesitation. "The application is denied," he said. "I find that the evidence is legally sufficient to support each of the charges set forth in the indictment."

As Marino assembled his papers to leave for the day, he was organizing his thoughts for his strategy for Oliver's defense. Marino's two key witnesses held the psychological evidence that could convince the jury that Oliver was mentally impaired. He would have to depend on his experts to save Oliver from being charged with second-degree murder.

Chapter 22:
OCTOBER 3, 1989
"I OWE OLIVER A FAIR TRIAL"

In the quiet of his own cluttered office, Nick Marino began to scan pages of notes he had taken over the past year on Oliver and his case.

During his cross-examinations of Detectives Donnelly and Parpan, he had tried to suggest that Oliver had been treated like a suspect from the moment the police arrived at his house, and that he had been wrongfully coerced into confessing. He hoped the jury would be sympathetic to these issues.

Now it was his turn to take center stage, to question witnesses brought in for the defense, and to introduce enough evidence to convince the jury that Oliver was not responsible for his actions on the night of September 24, 1988.

As the sun set behind the building and it was becoming more difficult to read his notes, Marino flicked on the office light, returned to his desk, and continued to study the papers in front of him.

Reading over a copy of the letter Oliver had written soon after his parents' death to "Tatoe," Oliver's own variation of the Yugoslavian word for "father," Marino genuinely believed that Oliver had expected an answer to his letter, and that he truly hadn't understood that his father was gone forever.

As Marino glanced at some of the drawings Oliver had sent him over the past few months, he smiled. There were sketches of him in action in the courtroom, others of Dan Cotter, of Judge Thorp, and of Oliver himself. Some resembled cartoons, others were more realistic renditions. In both forms they showed artistic talent that had probably always been buried deep within Oliver Petrovich. "What a waste," Marino mumbled to himself as he put the sketches into an envelope.

In the silence of his empty office Marino thought back to several different conversations he had had with Oliver about his parents over the past twelve months. Oliver's thoughts had been so inconsistent that sometimes it seemed impossible that they could have come from the mind of the same person.

Several times Oliver had told him that it was really his father he had hated, but he didn't know how he could have killed his mother who had been so good to him. Other times, often in the same week, he had cursed his mother for betraying him and cried over the loss of his father, who Oliver said had really only wanted the best for him.

One afternoon Oliver admitted to Marino that he was glad he had killed his parents, and the next day he cried that he missed them both so badly, he didn't know how he could go on without them.

While Marino reread some of the letters, he pictured Oliver's pitiful face just hours before, when they said good-bye to each other in the courtroom. He had seemed like a small child, confused and overwhelmed by what was going on around him.

Marino remembered well the unresponsive and distrusting Oliver he had met just about a year ago, and he thought about how their relationship had evolved over the year. Oliver had become eager to cooperate with him and had put all of his faith and trust into his expertise as a lawyer. Sometimes it was hard for Marino to make the connection that this defeated young man had actually murdered his parents. He felt now that he had an obligation, at the very least, to make sure he did his best to insure Oliver a fair trial.

For many hours over the past year he had read letters from Oliver and listened to painful stories of how his father had beaten him for no reason, of how hard he had always tried to please his father and how much he had feared him. Oliver had shared with him detailed accounts of how he had tortured animals and had once thrown a brick at a defenseless classmate's head.

But he had also told him about tender moments with Angel, how he had cared for her and how much he loved her. As Oliver had continued to confide in him, Marino had seen him as a tormented young man, and had understood the growing inner turmoil that had culminated on the night of September 24, 1988, with a furious battle between his heart and his mind. Oliver had told him all about that battle that tore his body apart until he ultimately made the decision to kill his parents.

When Marino looked down at his watch he was surprised to see how late it was. In just a few hours it would be time to present the psychological evidence that would show the jury that Oliver Petrovich was a young man who had a severe personality disorder, who couldn't handle stress, who had limited intellectual and reasoning abilities, who hadn't understood the Miranda rights that were given to him, and who didn't understand the consequences of his actions when he killed his parents.

Marino turned out the lights in his office and locked up to go home. He was feeling more optimistic that there was enough evidence to find Oliver severely emotionally disturbed, and he was hopeful that even if the jury found him guilty of the crime, they would convict him not of second-degree murder, but of the lesser charge of manslaughter.

Chapter 23:
OCTOBER 4, 1989
"IN YOUR EXPERT OPINION . . ."

"Dr. Klein, do you determine IQ levels as a result of the Wechsler Intelligence Test?" Marino asked his witness.

"Yes, I do," the psychologist answered.

"Could you explain to the ladies and gentlemen of the jury what IQ levels you determined Oliver Petrovich to have, as a result of administering this test?"

With professional ease, Alan Klein proceeded to explain that a score of 100 would generally be accepted as the average level IQ, with two thirds of the general population having IQ scores within the range of 90 to

110. A score above 110 is considered bright normal, and above 120 would be defined as superior intelligence. On the other end of the scale, a score between 80 and 90 would be considered dull normal, from 70 to 80 would be borderline defective and below 70 would be classified as defective. He then explained that the overall IQ score is a combination of verbal intelligence and performance intelligence.

Marino, approaching the witness, asked him to share with the jury the IQ scores of Oliver Petrovich.

Dr. Klein reported Oliver's verbal IQ at 79, which would be considered a borderline score and would indicate that he had difficulties in reasoning, acquiring information, and using abstract thinking. His performance IQ, on the other hand, was 112, within the average range of ability, and reflected Oliver's good mechanical and manipulative abilities.

When Marino asked Dr. Klein how stress would have affected Oliver's ability to respond to a situation, he answered that it would have substantially decreased it.

Marino was depending on Dr. Klein to recount the conversations he had had with Oliver, to present a picture of a severely emotionally disturbed young man who could not deal with the stress in his life, and who ultimately was not legally responsible for his actions on the night he shot his parents.

As directed, Dr. Klein discussed the relationship between Oliver and Karlene and how Oliver had sneaked her into his room and tried to conceal her presence from his parents.

When Marino asked Dr. Klein to discuss the relationship Oliver had with his parents, he described it as emotionally complicated. He explained that Oliver saw his mother as helpful and emotionally supportive, but his relationship with his father was an extremely conflicted one. Oliver often had described his father as someone who tormented him. If Oliver's mother sided with his father, Oliver felt that she too was tormenting him.

Dr. Klein described the different sides of Oliver's relationship with his father. On one hand he was filled with a desire to be accepted and liked by his father, but at the same time he had a sense of anxiety over his ability to meet his father's demands and had intense feelings of anger toward his father. Despite the conflicting emotions, Oliver had always tried, over the years, to meet his father's demands and requirements.

Marino led his questioning to the night of September 24, 1988, and Dr. Klein described to the jury Oliver's conflicts, increased stress, anxiety, and fearfulness. His concern that Karlene's discovery by his parents would leave them unable to continue their relationship created a state of mind in Oliver in which he could only see his parents as an obstacle. As his anxiety level climbed, he arrived at the conclusion that the only way he could resolve the situation was by removing the obstacle.

Finally Marino moved in for what he hoped would be his most important defense.

"Dr. Klein, with respect to the time that Oliver Petrovich shot his parents on the evening in question, do you have an expert opinion as a forensic psychologist whether or not he suffered at such time from a mental disease and/or disorder?"

"Yes, I do," the witness replied.

"And do you have an expert opinion as to whether

or not that mental disease and/or disorder resulted in his conduct?''

"Yes, I do.''

"And what is that opinion, sir?'' Marino asked.

"That the nature of his personality organization and personality disorder which he suffered from created a situation in which his reasoning abilities were so limited, his emotional state was so intense, that this solution appeared to be the only one available to him and the only action that he could take at the time.''

As Marino continued to question Dr. Klein on Oliver's mental state, the witness responded that Oliver had limited mental capacity and limited understanding of any future consequences.

He testified that in his expert opinion, Oliver was unable to appreciate the effect of his behavior and saw it only as an immediate solution to an immediate problem. In fact, he said, Oliver didn't understand that the next day his parents would not be there.

Finally Marino addressed the issue of Oliver's confession and asked Dr. Klein if he felt Oliver had understood the nature and consequences of remaining silent or giving a statement to the police.

Dr. Klein replied that while Oliver heard the words and was familiar with the phrases, he was not aware of what the long-term consequences of his behavior would be.

"If it wasn't for the use of Karlene Francis,'' Marino questioned him, "do you have an opinion as to whether Oliver Petrovich would have given the police the statement they were seeking?''

"My opinion is that but for the intervention of Miss Francis, Mr. Petrovich would not have made that statement.''

* * *

Dan Cotter was unwilling to allow Oliver to be pictured as someone who didn't appreciate the nature and consequence of his conduct. On cross-examination he asked Dr. Klein, "Do you believe that the defendant, when he shot his mother and shot his father, didn't know that they were going to be dead from that shooting?"

"I don't think that he really understood what that meant in terms of the future acts and future consequences."

"You mean the fact that he might go to jail as a result of this?" Cotter pushed.

"No," Klein replied. "In terms of the finality of the loss of his parents. I think he saw it as an immediate solution to an immediate problem and did not realize its finality."

But Cotter had just gotten started. "When he put the gun to the back of his mother's head, did he know that if he pulled that trigger, she would die?"

"Yes."

"Is there any doubt in your mind about that?"

"No."

"He knew, did he not, that he was putting a gun, and not a fork to the back of her head?" His voice was getting louder.

"Yes," Klein responded.

"He knew, did he not," Cotter persisted, "that it was a loaded gun, because you know that he checked it to make sure it was loaded before he did that?"

"That is correct."

"So he knew the nature of his act?"

"Correct."

"And he knew the immediate consequences of pulling the trigger would be what, Doctor?"

"The death of his mother."

"Doctor, is there any doubt in your mind that Oliver Petrovich, at the time he pointed the shotgun at his father's head, knew that it was a loaded gun?"

"No, there is no doubt."

"Is there any doubt in your mind that he knew the consequences of pulling the trigger at that time?"

"The immediate consequences."

"The immediate consequences at that time, in his mind, would be what?"

"That his father would die."

"Well, Doctor, he had been planning this for months. This wasn't something that popped into his mind that night, is it? Do you know that Vincent Wilson came into this courtroom and confirmed that months earlier the defendant had asked him for a gun with a silencer, to kill his father? And are you aware that in his statement, it's alleged that the defendant told the detective that he was planning to lure his parents to the apartment building in Flushing, so he could kill them there and make it look like a robbery?"

Although Dr. Klein could not dispute the facts, he did not waver in his impression that Oliver would not have committed the act of murder, regardless of the thoughts and comments he had made, if on that particular night his mother had not told his father about Karlene Francis living there and being hidden in that house over the preceding six months.

In spite of Cotter's strong cross-examination, Nick Marino felt that the case for the defense had gained ground with the testimony of Alan Klein. As Marino called his next witness, he was hopeful that Roger Feldman would present additional supportive psychological evidence that would further help Oliver's defense.

After Roger Feldman identified himself as a licensed physician and a practicing psychiatrist since 1971, Marino offered him to the Court and the jury as an expert with regard to issues concerning legal responsibility. Feldman told the Court that he had examined Oliver on two occasions, for the purpose of establishing his awareness of the nature of the offenses against him. Their first meeting was to develop a sense of Oliver's personality pattern, his style of thinking and behavior, and to explore his past history. The second interview focused more on the events around the deaths of his parents.

Marino began his questioning about Oliver's history with his parents. Dr. Feldman responded that Oliver had presented himself as a young man with an unhappy and troubled background. Oliver had painted a picture of a father who was very domineering, very controlling, critical, and possessive, who was both physically and mentally abusive. It was not uncommon for Oliver or his mother to be punched in the face when he was displeased.

Dr. Feldman proceeded to describe Oliver's allegiance with his mother, his feeling of not being loved or cared about by his father. He added that in public school Oliver had a pattern of fighting, emotional problems, difficulty learning, and poor relationships with other children.

When Marino asked about Oliver's relationships with others, Dr. Feldman explained that Oliver was limited socially and had very few meaningful friends.

His only longstanding relationships were delinquent in nature.

But when Marino introduced the subject of Karlene Francis and Oliver's relationship with her, Dr. Feldman explained that their immediate bond was based on the unhappiness they had in common. As two outcasts, they connected with each other, and as Oliver became extremely attached to Karlene, he needed to be with her more and more.

Marino continued to lead the witness. "How do you reconcile the fact, Doctor, that here is an individual who had these problems with his father, yet he hides a black girl in his house against his parents' wishes?"

"Well, I think Oliver has always been a very angry man, and there has always been a great deal of rage at his father whom he saw as so cruel and sadistic. But one thing he could not do was to be angry with that kind of father. He could never stand up to his father. So what better way to get back at his father but to do something that would be a way of kind of laughing at him on one hand, but also doing something that he knows is rebellious. That was the only way that Oliver could show his anger at his father."

"Doctor," Marino challenged the witness, "wouldn't that be risky to Oliver Petrovich, in terms of his fear of his father?"

"Oliver liked risks," Dr. Feldman replied. "Much of his life involved taking risks—in cars, on motor scooters, jumping on trains. There was a history of risk-taking in his life, so that was one thing that gave him his sense of control and a sense of doing something that made him strong."

Marino directed his questioning to the night Oliver shot his parents. "Did you come to an opinion as to whether Oliver Petrovich, on the day he shot his mother and father, was suffering from a mental disease or defect or disorder?"

"Oliver has a severe character disorder," the psychiatrist answered thoughtfully. "He was a very infantile, dependent, weak young man, who didn't have the capacity to cope with many of life's stresses or problems, and certainly didn't have the capacity to cope with the conflict he faced that night. When he heard that Angel would have to leave, his life kind of crumbled because he had to make a decision. He had to either give up the girl or leave home, and he was not prepared to do either one. So he was thrown into a crisis and he went into a state of panic.

"Then it occurred to him that the only solution was to kill his parents. Somehow, that would magically solve the problem and that's how children solve problems—by magic. Magically, somehow, if he killed his parents, then everything would be solved. It was only for the moment. If they're gone right now, this minute, then there won't be any more problem. He didn't think about tomorrow, the next day, or anything else.

"So, in his state of panic he was struggling. What should he do? Should he kill them? Shouldn't he kill them? Was it right or wrong? He was in this state for hours, kind of wandering around the house. Getting the gun, putting the gun away. Trying to work out in his own mind a solution. Eventually, at a moment of extreme agitation, he killed them. Of course it wrecked his life, but that was the answer at that moment."

Marino paced back and forth between the witness stand and the jury. He was pleased with the effectiveness of Feldman's testimony, but he still had several more points to cover.

He needed to zero in on Oliver's capacity to appreciate the nature and consequences of his conduct. As he had hoped, Dr. Feldman testified that Oliver was not fully aware that he was actually killing his parents —that although he knew it was wrong and he knew the immediate consequences, he believed that the next day would be another day, and he would get up and talk to his parents again.

Marino's confidence in the testimonies of his expert witnesses was growing. Before he finished questioning Dr. Feldman, he wanted to eliminate the motive of greed from the jury's minds.

"Dr. Feldman," he asked, "is it your opinion that Oliver Petrovich shot and killed his parents to get the house and any other assets, an apartment building or the property that they may have owned?"

"It is my opinion that that wasn't in his mind. The only thing in his mind was losing Karlene."

When psychologist Laura Edwards, a witness for the People, took the stand and was asked by Dan Cotter about her two interviews with Oliver Petrovich and her evaluation of psychological tests that she had administered, she described an Oliver Petrovich that sounded nothing like the young man presented by the Defense.

"Throughout the process of test taking I was able to converse with Mr. Petrovich," Dr. Edwards said, "and he was very friendly, very open, and a lot of times we paused with the testing because there were things he wanted to chat about."

Based on the results of the IQ test that Dr. Edwards

administered, the same Wechsler Adult Intelligence Scale–Revised that had been used by Dr. Klein, Oliver's verbal IQ score was calculated to be 89, and his performance IQ score to be 98, which she said when combined placed him well within the normal average range.

"Now, Doctor," Cotter asked, "during your interviews, what was the defendant's demeanor when you first met him and began your interviews and tests?"

"He was very pleasant, very courteous, very polite," she answered. "He seemed to like the attention. He asked me if I had followed his case in the press and he seemed very disappointed when I indicated to him that I tend not to read criminal accounts in the paper, because very often I might become involved in the case, and I really don't want to be biased by the press." She paused, then added, "He asked me a lot of personal questions. He wanted to know all about me."

After Cotter finished questioning Dr. Edwards about Oliver's ability to understand his Miranda rights and received the answers he was seeking ("In my opinion, Oliver Petrovich did not suffer from a mental disease or defect which rendered him substantially incapable of understanding the consequences of his actions or that they were wrong"), he called to the stand Alfred Dolgin, a forensic psychiatrist and another witness for the People.

Dr. Dolgin had examined Oliver to determine whether he was legally responsible for his actions.

"Doctor," Cotter asked, "based on your examinations of all the materials and your interviews with Mr. Petrovich, what is your opinion with respect to whether or not Mr. Petrovich, at the time of the shootings, knew and appreciated the consequences of his acts?"

"My opinion is that Mr. Petrovich appreciated quite well the consequences of his conduct."

"And did you form an opinion," Cotter continued, "on the threshold question as to whether or not he had a mental disease or defect?"

"There was no important mental disturbance so that I found loss of contact with reality," Dr. Dolgin answered. "He was aware of what was going on around him. He knew where he was, who he was with. He knew it was a gun, he knew it fired bullets. He had the capacity, and he knew it would cause death if used in a certain way."

Back and forth Cotter and Marino took their respective turns to question the witnesses, cross-examine, re-question and re-cross-examine. They debated technical issues, both hoping to win points with the jury.

Finally both the People and the Defense rested their cases, and Judge Thorp announced to the jury that the presentation of evidence at the trial had been concluded. After the jury was dismissed for the day, the judge held a conference in his chambers with both attorneys, relative to the charge to be delivered to the jury.

"Mr. Marino," Judge Thorp asked, "with respect to each of the two counts of the indictment, do you request that I instruct the jury to consider the affirmative defense of extreme emotional disturbance, reducing murder in the second degree to manslaughter in the first degree?"

"I do, Your Honor," Marino answered. "In whatever order the Court feels it follows or is in conjunction with the charges of 'not responsible by mental disease and/or defect.' "

The judge agreed to instruct the jury that if they unanimously found the defendant guilty, they must consider, in addition to the charge of second-degree murder, the defense of extreme emotional disturbance, which would reduce the charge to manslaughter.

Marino left the judge's chambers with renewed hope for his client. But the next morning his hopes were shattered by Oliver himself. After more than a year of cooperating with Marino and trusting his legal expertise, Oliver Petrovich had suddenly decided to think for himself.

Chapter 24:
OCTOBER 11–12, 1989
"WE HAVE REACHED THE VERDICTS"

Nick Marino was laying out his papers in preparation for his summation when Oliver leaned over to him and whispered in his ear. Bewildered by Oliver's request, Marino approached the judge.

"Your Honor," he addressed Judge Thorp, "my client has just indicated to me that he is requesting a five-minute or so temporary stay of the starting of this trial this morning, so he can consult with me and explain certain things to me that he wishes to do."

"Granted," the judge responded.

When they returned ten minutes later, Marino's face was drained of all color. His client had just informed him that he refused to allow the jury to consider a verdict of manslaughter. Oliver insisted that if the jury had manslaughter on the verdict sheet, they would compromise and come in with that.

Marino shook his head in defeat. Minutes before, he had been prepared to sum up the case on issues of insanity and extreme emotional disturbance. Oliver's sudden decision had taken him by surprise.

Judge Thorp, as surprised by Oliver's sudden change of heart as Marino himself, listened sympathetically to Marino's request that he override the defendant's decision and submit the consideration of manslaughter to the jury.

"There is a reasonable view of the evidence that supports such a submission," Judge Thorp agreed with Marino. "However, in the last analysis, it is the client you represent who has to make the decision." To give Marino a further opportunity to consult with Oliver, the judge called for a short recess. But even behind closed doors with his attorney, Oliver remained adamant about his position and refused to listen to Marino's reasoning.

While he stared straight ahead, Oliver was thinking about Joe Morelo, one of his fellow inmates, who had persuaded him to drop the manslaughter charge from the choices. If it hadn't been for Joe, Oliver probably would have followed Marino's lead and gone after the lesser conviction. But since meeting Joe, Oliver had been impressed with how much he knew about law. Having followed Oliver's trial from the beginning, Joe told Oliver that he could get off on an insanity plea and that if he settled for less he'd be selling out.

Oliver was, and always had been, a risk-taker. He didn't want any part of a lesser conviction. For better or for worse, he decided to go for it. Now there was no turning back.

In the courtroom, Judge Thorp summoned Oliver to the bench in order to speak to him. He reminded Oliver that, just the day before, they had confirmed the submission to the jury of the additional defense of extreme emotional disturbance, which would reduce the charge of second-degree murder to that of first-degree manslaughter.

"You were in the courtroom yesterday when I made that statement," Judge Thorp said to Oliver. "Is that correct?"

"Yeah," Oliver answered in a monotone, "but I didn't understand what was going on, you know—"

Judge Thorp interrupted him. "What do you mean you don't understand what is going on? If I submit the case to the jury in that fashion—"

This time it was Oliver who interrupted the judge. "In what way?"

"In the way I announced yesterday, which was in accordance with Mr. Marino's request. With respect to each charge there would be four possible verdicts: guilty of murder in the second degree, guilty of manslaughter in the first degree, not responsible by reason of mental disease or defect, or not guilty."

Oliver shook his head. "I want it down to three choices," he said. "I didn't do any crime in my right mind."

Marino, obviously distraught over Oliver's reaction, tried to clarify his client's confusion. "He is completely misunderstanding that the submission of one does not mean the exclusion of the other," he told Judge Thorp. "And that's where Oliver and I have not linked this morning." He hoped that the Court could make Oliver realize that his decision was a serious mistake.

The judge nodded and reexplained to Oliver the various submissions and what each meant.

He emphasized the difference between a conviction of second-degree murder, which meant twenty-five years to life for each count of murder, and a conviction of first-degree manslaughter based on extreme emotional disturbance, which would reduce the sentence for each charge to between eight-and-a third and twenty-five years. He then asked Oliver, "Did Mr. Marino already explain to you the possible sentences which you could receive, were you convicted of murder in the second degree?"

"Yeah," Oliver answered, looking down at the floor.

"Did he explain to you the possible sentences you could receive if you were convicted of manslaughter in the first degree?"

Again, Oliver responded with a barely audible, "Yeah."

"And you're aware that there is a significant difference in the severity of the sentences?" the judge asked him.

Oliver looked up at the judge and said, "Well, if I get out at age forty, how much longer am I going to live? Three—"

An interruption was heard from Cotter, who was growing impatient with this discussion. He pointed out to the judge that more than an hour had already lapsed in delays, and he felt that it was time to make a decision and begin the summations.

But Marino, still shaking his head in disbelief, insisted that he could not proceed with this matter unresolved, as he had prepared his summation based on the inclusion of the charge of manslaughter.

Judge Thorp granted another recess to give Marino a final opportunity to talk to Oliver, to try to persuade him to change his mind.

It was after eleven when Judge Thorp again addressed Oliver.

"Mr. Petrovich, in the last analysis it's your decision that controls your attorney's actions. Mr. Marino has indicated that you wish not to follow his advice and have me submit to the jury the possible verdict of guilty of first-degree manslaughter. Is that what you wish?"

"Yeah," Oliver answered.

"That's your decision?"

"Yes."

Turning to Marino, Judge Thorp said with finality, "Mr. Marino, the law is clear that an attorney advises his client. The client makes the decisions. I have no choice."

At 11:25 A.M. the jury entered the courtroom and prepared to hear the summations from both attorneys. Under court procedures, the defense counsel was called to sum up first.

"Honorable Justice Thorp, Mr. Cotter, and forelady of the jury, ladies and gentlemen of the jury, good morning," Marino began. "Ladies and gentlemen, we have had a fairly lengthy trial here. We are into our third week. Now we have come to the issues of finalizing this case once and for all. . . . ."

For the next hour and a half Marino spoke passionately to the members of the jury, making eye contact with each and talking to them as if he knew them all personally. In his defense for Oliver, he didn't want to minimize the tragedy of the deaths of Mr. and Mrs. Petrovich, and he emphasized the dreadful proportions of the situation, in which, he said, there was no winner.

Marino asked the jurors to put themselves into the shoes of Oliver Petrovich, to try to understand what was happening in his life not only on the day of September 24, 1988, but for six months before, and many years before that.

He referred again to Dr. Feldman's testimony that Oliver was an infantile, childlike individual, thinking that he was solving a problem for the moment.

"I submit to you, ladies and gentlemen, that Oliver Petrovich is not guilty of murder. I submit to you that the D.A. has not proved the issue of intent. That this was a situation that was developing into a crisis beyond Oliver's control."

Marino knew that this was his final opportunity to present every possible argument for Oliver. Once again he referred to Oliver's confession, insisting that it had not been given voluntarily, was taken in violation of Oliver's constitutional rights, and should be disregarded. He submitted that Oliver's statement had been obtained by the use of improper conduct by the police department and undue pressure by the police which had impaired Oliver's mental condition to the extent of undermining his ability to make the choice of whether or not to make the statement.

Marino looked over at Oliver, whose head was down on the table in front of him.

"Ladies and gentlemen," he continued, "this case is all about a young man who lived in a home where he was alienated . . . There was no love. There was no affection. There was no sentiment between parent and child. This is how this young man grew up. He not only has a low IQ, but failing grades in school and low comprehension. . . . All of the factors of Oliver Petrovich's background cannot be ignored because they are building blocks; they are the foundation upon which the tragic event developed. . . .

"Remember the death threats to Oliver Petrovich by his father with regard to a black girlfriend. Not once, not twice, but a number of times. And there is the gun and the ammunition to carry out these threats. This is a father who physically and mentally abused his child. That's what leads to explosions. There is a set of circumstances that develop, not mandated or planned by this individual, but they just happen to be there, and they culminate. They get triggered. The bubble bursts. . . .

"Dr. Edwards testified that Oliver was disappointed that another case had gotten more TV coverage than his, that he was trying to look good for the TV cameras. Is that indicative of a man capable of abstract reasoning and rational thought, who understood the nature and consequences of his acts and his surroundings? Or is that a man who is lost in Never-Never Land? . . .

"Oliver Petrovich's thoughts about killing his parents were like a child's, like a fantasy. His life crumbled. He was forced to give up his girlfriend and/or leave home, and he couldn't do both. For a while he couldn't make the choice. He wrestled and wrestled, and Karlene, his only source of support, came home, and then Oliver Petrovich pulled the trigger. At the time in question Oliver Petrovich was laboring under an emotion that was panic. He was frightened and vulnerable. He became extremely anxious. Agitated. And then he found a magic resolution—on a temporary basis, only for the moment—to remove his obstacle, his parents, without any thought or appreciation as to the consequences, the permanence, the result of what he was doing. He had no idea that the next morning they wouldn't be there. Yes, it's a thin line. But I respectfully submit to you, ladies and gentlemen, that this thin line has been crossed here. . . .

"After you have deliberated and really narrowed the case down to the issues at hand, there will be but one verdict that is in conformance with the evidence or lack thereof, and I respectfully submit to you that you will come back to this courtroom and indicate that Oliver Petrovich is not guilty of the crimes to which he is charged. Thank you very much for your kind attention this morning."

After a lunch recess Dan Cotter was called by the court to present his summation on behalf of the People.

"If it pleases the Court, Judge Thorp, Mr. Marino, ladies and gentlemen of the jury," he said as he approached the jury box. "This is my last opportunity to address you, to talk to you about the evidence, about the charges in this case, and indicate to you how I feel the evidence has proved the crimes charged in the indictment itself."

In his straightforward, no-nonsense style, Cotter

submitted to the jury that the People had proved through all of the evidence that when Oliver Petrovich shot both of his parents, he knew exactly what he was doing.

"Did he know that he was picking up a gun or a fork? That sounds like a silly example, but if you want to make a phone call, do you walk over and open the refrigerator door, or do you walk over and pick up the telephone?"

He reminded the jury that they were there to determine whether Oliver had intentionally killed.

"Was it a mistake?" he asked the jurors. "Did he only mean to injure them? He went and got a shotgun and went upstairs so his father wouldn't hear him, and he checked to make sure there were three bullets in it. Then he practiced aiming it, practiced loading it, checked the safety to make sure it worked, and he used this to go down and kill both his parents. Is that an insane person?"

Again he advised them that if they found that Oliver had intentionally shot his parents and caused their death, then he was guilty of murder.

Cotter then addressed the issue of insanity, and insisted to the jury that there was not one shred of evidence to indicate that Oliver was insane.

"When you put a gun to the back of somebody's head and you pull the trigger, the natural consequences are that the gun is going to be discharged and there is going to be nothing left of that person's head. He is going to die."

He reminded the jury of Oliver's conversation with Vincent Wilson, in which he asked his co-worker to get him a gun because he wanted to kill his father.

"Did he say, can you give me a fork? No, he said,

can you get me a gun. Something that will kill. Not only did he say get me a gun, but get me a gun with a silencer, so that when I do it, I want to get away with it."

Cotter urged the jury not to consider Oliver insane, but a criminal committing criminal acts, trying to conceal evidence, concoct an alibi, and lie. He urged them to listen to Oliver's videotaped confession, to hear Oliver's own chilling version of what he did.

"And he says on the videotape after being asked, when his mother screamed, what did he do? In about as cold-blooded a response as you're ever going to get, he said, 'I shot her in the head.' And then when he is asked about his father, he said, 'I shot him a second time. I aimed at his head and I shot him.' "

After forty minutes—a short summation compared to Marino's—Cotter closed by thanking the jury for their patience and attention during the trial, and asked them to render a fair, impartial verdict based on the facts and evidence in the case. Exhausted from his summation but confident that the presentation had been effective, he returned slowly to his seat.

"Ladies and gentlemen," Judge Thorp addressed the jury, "trial by jury in criminal cases is the very foundation stone of the true administration of justice in our society. It is a means by which we calmly, rationally, and objectively try to arrive at the truth in a given situation."

Judge Thorp reminded the jury once again of the presumption of innocence until a defendant's guilt is established beyond a reasonable doubt. He reminded them of their duty to determine the facts, and at the same time to accept the law of the case as given to them by the Court. "Whatever your verdict may be in this case," he continued, "it must be a unanimous vote. Each of you twelve members of the jury must individually agree on the verdict. You must each decide the case for yourself. . . . You are expected to confer, exchange ideas, listen to your fellow jurors with an open mind, but while remembering that each of you must individually decide the case."

The judge warned the jury not to base their verdict on sympathy, or upon what the reaction to their verdict might be.

"There is no magic formula by which one may evaluate testimony," he said. "Each of you brings with you to this courtroom all of the experience and background of your own lives. In your everyday affairs you determine for yourselves the reliability or unreliability of statements made to you by others. . . . You may reject an expert's opinion if you find the facts upon which he or she based it to be different from your understanding of the facts. You may also reject an expert's opinion if, after carefully considering all the evidence in the case, you disagree with the expert."

Before he dismissed the jury, Judge Thorp reviewed again the term "reasonable doubt," and cautioned the jury that if a reasonable doubt existed, they must give the benefit of that doubt to the defendant and acquit him. If no reasonable doubt was found to exist, he added, it was equally their duty to convict.

Once again he explained the charges and the elements necessary for conviction. When he had completed his charges to the jury and was satisfied that he had prepared them for their task ahead, he concluded, "You may now retire to commence your deliberations."

* * *

At 5:01 P.M. the jury left the courtroom. At 6:56 they recessed for the night and were taken out to a local restaurant for dinner, after which they were given rooms at a nearby motel and adjourned until the next morning.

During the following morning of October 12 the jury, split in their decision, requested both the taped and written confessions for review, and asked for further clarification on the law pertaining to the insanity plea. With a unanimous vote necessary, their deliberations continued into the afternoon.

Oliver Petrovich and Nick Marino sat together, absently drinking coffee, restlessly waiting for further news. Dan Cotter continued to look at his watch, also anxious for word from the jury. Each was lost in his own private thoughts when the clerk handed a note to Judge Thorp and the judge announced, "We have a note from the jury. It reads, 'We have reached the verdicts.'"

Chapter 25: OCTOBER 12, 1989—THE PRESENT

"MY LITTLE ANGEL"

"Madam Forelady, has the jury reached a verdict?" the clerk asked.

"Yes," the forelady responded.

"Madam forelady, what is your verdict as to the first count?" he questioned.

"Guilty of murder in the second degree."

"Madam forelady, what is your verdict as to the second count?"

"Guilty of murder in the second degree," she repeated.

The clerk spoke. "Hearken as you hear the verdict

recorded. You say you find the defendant, Oliver Petrovich, guilty of murder in the second degree under the first count, and guilty of murder in the second degree under the second count. Is that your verdict, so say you all?"

All of the jurors answered in unison, "Yes."

Judge Thorp dismissed the jury at 5:10 P.M. and announced that Oliver Petrovich would be sentenced on November 13, 1989, and would be held until that date, without bail, at the Nassau County Jail.

The next afternoon Oliver called Detective Parpan collect at police headquarters and was surprisingly in a very good mood.

"I guess it was close, huh, detective?" he asked Parpan. "After all, the jury was out overnight."

"Sure, Oliver," Parpan answered, baffled by Oliver's cheerfulness. "Oliver," he asked, "why did you decide to drop the charge of manslaughter?"

"Well," he answered slowly, "the other night as I was getting out of the shower I ran into a jailhouse lawyer. And he told me it was a bad compromise— that I had a good shot at getting off on insanity."

"But Oliver," Parpan persisted, "you dealt with Nick Marino for over a year. Why didn't you listen to him?"

"I don't know." Oliver's voice had lost some of its enthusiasm. "I guess I really believed I'd get off."

On November 13 Judge Thorp issued his sentence for Oliver Petrovich. In his statement the judge said that Oliver had plotted the murder of his parents in a chillingly calculated way, and he gave him the maximum term of fifty years to life imprisonment.

Oliver stood mutely, listening with his eyes down-
cast and no expression on his face. He refused even to
acknowledge his name when spoken to.

Marino had submitted lengthy pleas to Judge Thorp
—one to modify the term on the grounds that Oliver
was a disturbed young man who exploded when his
parents rejected his girlfriend Karlene. But Judge
Thorp noted that Oliver himself had asked the jury not
to consider the lesser charge of first-degree manslaughter. Marino had also pleaded that the judge consider the acts of murder as a single crime, and that he
sentence him to two twenty-five-year to life terms to
be served concurrently, instead of consecutively,
which would double his minimum time. But Judge
Thorp rejected that plea as well.

"He shot both his parents in cold blood after first
attempting to strangle his mother," the judge said.
"The jury in its decision rejected the psychiatric testimony and convicted the defendant of second-degree
murder on each count."

Before the court was adjourned, Judge Thorp
granted a request for protective custody and a suicide
watch on Oliver.

Oliver spent the next two months at the Nassau
County Jail. Shortly after his sentencing he was hit on
the head with a mop handle while he was sleeping,
and needed sixteen stitches on his ear. The inmate
who hit him, a burly black teenager, had just been
looking for something exciting to do.

After Oliver returned to his floor from the infirmary,
he asked if he could call home. He tried to explain to
the warden, "I have to call my parents to tell them
what happened."

Several times Oliver tried to call home collect to speak to his parents. When there was no answer he was confused. "Maybe my father's not home from work yet," he told the guard with him. "And my mom can't hear the phone because she's watering the garden out front."

The night after one of his unanswered phone calls, Oliver, still obsessed with the need to see and speak to his parents, dreamed that he went to their graves, dug them both up, and opened their coffins. He was finally wakened from his nightmare by his own loud cries.

The next morning Oliver looked into the bathroom mirror and, crying again, asked himself out loud, "What did you do, Oliver? You're in here for murder! How could you have murdered your parents?"

Every day Oliver woke up in jail to the same emptiness. He looked forward to food and sleep; there was nothing more. He kept to himself, and avoided contact with the other inmates.

"If I ever get out of here," he told a guard one day, "maybe I'll stay away from women, and be married to a car instead."

But from early morning until he finally fell asleep at night, he couldn't stop thinking about Angel. Since the sentencing she hadn't visited him but had sent him several letters. When his mind wandered to the times they had together, Oliver remembered how happy she had made him feel, and he ached to touch her, to hold her; he longed for her body under his. When thoughts of suicide invaded his mind, the image of his beautiful Angel was the only force strong enough to push the idea away.

Oliver wrote a letter to Nick Marino and asked if he could arrange it so that he and Angel could get married. "If we were married, we could have trailer visits," he wrote in his letter. "And then I could get her pregnant and have a child to carry on my name. At least this way, if I get out at age fifty, I'll have a child."

But after writing the letter, Oliver ripped it up, knowing that it would never work. He knew that his dreams about Angel and himself were impossible, because Angel was already pregnant, but Oliver was not the father.

He had found out during the trial from a letter that Angel had mailed to him in jail, because she had been afraid to tell him in person. When he read the letter Oliver had felt the veins in his forehead start to throb. At first all he could think about was how he would kill Angel, and then kill himself.

For several days after he received her letter, Oliver had refused to eat or talk to anyone. He hadn't answered when he was called, and had behaved as if he were in a trance.

When Oliver spoke to Marino for the first time after learning of the news, he exploded over the phone.

"That bitch!" he shouted. "How could she have done that to me? I'll kill her, that nigger bitch!"

But when Marino told Oliver that he too had received a letter from Karlene telling him how much she still loved Oliver, his anger began to subside.

Talking calmly to Oliver, Marino said, "Don't put more pressure on her, Oliver. Life's too short as it is."

Somehow, those words were comforting to Oliver and he felt better.

Soon after the phone conversation with Marino other letters from Angel had arrived, explaining to Oliver how lonely she had been without him, how she had thought a baby would give her someone to love, to make her feel important. And above all, now that she was pregnant she could live for free in a home for unwed mothers.

She apologized for hurting him, promised that she still loved him and would never cheat on him again, vowed that once the baby came she'd be too busy to fool around with other guys, and prayed that he would forgive her and still love her.

Gradually Oliver had grown to accept Angel's logic, and his anger subsided.

During another telephone conversation with Marino several weeks later he said, "You know, Mr. Marino, I hope Angel finds a guy to love, and he treats her better than I could. And most of all, I hope that his parents both love her."

On January 2, 1990, Oliver was transferred with twenty other inmates to Downstate Correctional Facility in Fishkill, New York, where he remained until May. Although he was not happy to have his head completely shaved, Oliver liked his temporary stay in the new prison where, six days after arriving, he quietly celebrated his twenty-fifth birthday. Oliver had told one of the guards that it was his birthday, and he brought a small cake into Oliver's cell. That night when the guards ordered out for Chinese food they brought Oliver a plate of sesame chicken for a special birthday dinner.

In his new home he had his own room with a window that he could open whenever he wanted to. The room had a tiled floor, a large mirror and its own light switch, instead of one central switch for the entire tier of cells. He was given a new set of clothes: several pairs of prison green pants and shirts, socks, sneakers, a pair of boots, and one coat.

At Downstate, Oliver passed his time feeding the birds out of his window. To earn privileges he worked in the laundry room, bringing in the cleaning. It was there that he started talking to another inmate who told Oliver that he was studying law. Oliver listened intently to the inmate's stories of past cases that he was studying. As his own interest in law grew, Oliver began to send for books from the library and to study the process of appealing a criminal conviction.

Marino had told him that in his best interests, a new lawyer was going to be assigned to handle his appeal, but Oliver hadn't yet heard from anyone or gotten any news. One of the first things he learned in his readings was that he could include a brief of his own in his appeal. The more he read up on past cases, the more Oliver became convinced that the police had violated his rights, and the more seriously he thought about preparing his own case for appeal.

On a cold and cloudy spring morning in mid-May, Oliver was told that he would be moving to a new home. Several officers holding sticks kept the thirty inmates in order on line while they waited to be handcuffed. When they were given the signal, the officers began the arduous procedure of handcuffing each inmate, pairing the inmates and shackling their ankles together, tying a chain around their waists and securing it to a master padlock. They slid a heavy metal black box over each set of handcuffs to lock them in place and prevent the prisoners from twisting their hands in front of them. They then locked the handcuffs to the waist chains to make sure the inmates couldn't strike one another on the bus, linked each man to a master 40-foot chain, and directed them to walk into the bus garage.

As Oliver dragged himself toward the garage he was thinking that escape would be impossible, because it would mean that all thirty men, handcuffed, shackled, and connected to one another, would have to be perfectly synchronized to move together.

Inside the garage a coach bus with tinted windows was ready for them. On both sides of the bus were the words "New York State Correctional Services." The bus driver, a twenty-year veteran for the state prisons, waited to be sure that his passengers were seated before starting on his journey. He knew that he had a long day ahead of him since he'd be stopping at three different prisons to deposit the designated inmates at each one. The last and farthest stop was the Clinton Correctional Facility, a maximum security prison in Dannemora, New York, near the Canadian border. Because of its inaccessibility and frigid winter temperatures, Clinton had earned the nickname "Siberia." It was to this prison that Oliver had been assigned.

Aboard the bus were two corrections officers whose job was to keep the inmates quiet. Unarmed to avoid the possibility of a mutiny, they sat among the prisoners, behind a window with steel bars that separated them from the driver and three other officers armed with shotguns.

During the six-hour bus trip Oliver occupied himself by looking out the window at the mountains and trees. His mind wandered from long-ago days of hunting with his father and begging his father to stop killing innocent animals, to the more recent evening when he had used the shotgun that he hated, to kill his own father.

When they finally reached Dannemora, Oliver was surprised to see that the two-part prison was right in the middle of a small town. The driver pulled into the first parking lot and one of the corrections officers removed the ankle shackles that connected Oliver to another inmate. Following the orders of a second officer, the inmates dragged themselves off the bus and were escorted into a large stone building. Only Oliver was instructed to remain seated on the bus.

Wasting no time, the driver exited through the main gate and, several hundred yards up the road, turned into another driveway. Facing Oliver, surrounded by a white three-story cement wall, was Clinton's maximum security prison, for inmates with long-term sentences.

As Oliver stood to get off the bus, he was wondering if he'd ever get out of prison, or if he'd grow old behind the white cement wall.

The Clinton Correctional Facility reminded Oliver of a jail out of the movies. Off the long hallways were small 5×7-foot cells with bars on the doors. A school bell woke the inmates every morning at 6 A.M. to give them time to get ready for breakfast.

The first time Oliver stepped out on his tier for a prison count, he heard another inmate shout out, "That's the guy that knocked off his parents!"

Unlike some of the prisoners, Oliver received no visitors. When he wasn't at mandatory gym twice a week or out in the yard for recreation time, he spent his days in his cell, researching more past criminal cases that he thought would be helpful for his appeal, taking pages of notes on what he learned, sketching scenes from prison and from memories of his past, writing letters to Nick Marino, to his newly assigned appeal lawyer, and to Angel.

He knew that it would be impossible for Angel to visit him in "Siberia." But he longed for her letters and looked forward to the mail every day, hoping that there would be something for him.

Soon after he arrived at Clinton, Oliver got the news that Karlene had given birth to a baby girl, whom she named Marianne. He had been waiting with mixed emotions for the announcement.

As Oliver read Karlene's letter informing him of Marianne's birth and describing the tiny baby, he felt a rush of pride, as if he were actually her father and the baby belonged to both of them. Marianne would be his little Angel.

As he breathed in the perfume from Angel's stationery, read her romantic words that told how she loved him, how she thought about him every day and still wanted to marry him, Oliver was filled with happiness and the promising dream that someday soon he'd win his appeal and be able to leave Dannemora and be reunited with his Angel. And then together, with their little Angel, they'd live happily ever after.

POSTSCRIPT

Oliver Petrovich, serving his sentence at maximum security Clinton Correctional Facility in Dannemora, New York, spends most of his time alone. Aside from an occasional letter from his cousin Terry, he has no contact with anyone from his family.

The inmates at Dannemora are given several choices for how to use their free time. At first Oliver signed up for drafting because he had always enjoyed drawing, but then he changed his mind to work in the prison tailor shop, so that he could earn money that he'd be allowed to use at the commissary. For twenty-nine cents an hour he works from Monday to Friday, from seven in the morning until three in the afternoon, at the tailor shop, where his responsibilities include stacking, ironing, and occasionally using a sewing machine for stitching coats and pants for inmates.

247

Every two weeks Oliver earns twenty dollars, with which he purchases snacks, pens, paper and other personal items.

Not interested in socializing, Oliver has made no effort to befriend any of his fellow inmates, except for one short, burly Greek man named Nick, who is also serving time for murder. When they sit together in the mess hall during mealtimes or at the movies on Friday and Saturday nights, they talk mostly about cars.

When he is not working or eating, Oliver chooses to spend his time alone in his cell. From another inmate he bought a set of headphones which can be plugged into an outlet in his cell that connects to a central recording room. With a choice of music or twenty-four-hour news, Oliver usually turns to "The Wizard of Rock."

Endless hours of solitude are broken up by reading Dick Tracy comics and daily newspapers. After reading in *Newsday* about another Long Island young man arrested for killing his parents, Oliver decided to write to the accused, with firsthand advice.

"I know what he's going through," Oliver told Nick one evening as he was heading back to his cell to start his letter. He outlined a detailed list of tips for how to help an attorney in jury selection, explained about the pre-trial hearings, and ended his letter with strong advice: "It's better to go for a manslaughter plea bargain."

In recent months Oliver has spent more of his time working on his own appeal. After studying Supreme Court rulings he has taken over 100 pages of notes on past cases. Obsessed with proving that his confession was illegally coerced and with collecting enough evidence to get his confession suppressed, Oliver has written numerous letters to Nick Marino, requesting information and copies of the testimonies of Detectives Parpan and Donnelly from his hearings.

While taking notes, Oliver often begins to daydream: about bringing Angel and Marianne to many of the places on Long Island where he used to go with Angel, and about being a cop. He fantasizes about dramatic shootouts and about arrests he would make. He pictures himself testifying in court. He imagines himself on patrol, picking up Marianne from school to take her with him for the rest of his shift. In his daydream they go together to pick up Angel when her shift is over at the hospital where she works as a nurse.

Oliver's dreams of living with Angel in the Great Neck house were shattered when he learned that the house had been sold. The estates of his parents, including the Flushing apartment and assets from the auction sale of the house, have been frozen, pending the outcome of Oliver's appeal. Until that time the Public Administrator of Nassau County will serve as temporary administrator of the estates, with a temporary trustee assigned to oversee the operations of the apartment building.

For over a year after the deaths of Anna and Svetozar Petrovich, the contents of their home were also held by the Public Administrator because of extensive delays in determining which side of the family was the beneficiary of the estate. Finally the furniture and other items from the Great Neck house were released to the relatives of Svetozar Petrovich, living in Yugoslavia.

Oliver was given authority over his personal possessions, including his car, which he released to Angel's sister because Angel had never learned to drive. His only request was that his car manuals and magazines be sent to him in Dannemora.

There is not much happiness in Oliver's life at the Clinton Correctional Facility. One day rolls into the next, and the only thing that lifts his spirits is the occasional letter from Angel.

In one of her most recent letters she wrote to him, "Oliver, you've been so good to me and I always took you for granted. I could never love anyone as I love you. You will always hold the key to my heart."

Sitting alone in his cell, hunched over the paper in front of him, Oliver wrote back to Angel, "All I have in my life now is my job, my appeal, and your love."

From Clinton Correctional Facility in Dannemora, New York, Oliver Petrovich sent to the author a series of 149 drawings, depicting scenes of his personal life over the years, from his early childhood to present. With Oliver's consent, the author chose from the series the following drawings to be included in this book.

AFTER MOM TELLS DAD ALL ABOUT ANGELS STAY HERE FOR 6-MONTHS, AND HOW I SNEAK HER IN AND OUT, AND AFTER MY DAD YELLED AND ARGUED WITH ME AND MY MOM, HE GRABBED THIS BLACK CLUB HE KEPT IN HIS ROOM, AND HE RAN UP TO MY ROOM TO CHECK MY CLOSET FOR ANGEL

POLICE HEADQUARTERS INTERROGATION PART-1

THE POLICE GOT ANGEL TO TRY TO PERSUADE OLIVER TO CONFESS THE KILLING, NAMELY, THIS IS B THE LADY DETECTIVES — IDEA, THE MEN DETECTIVES GO ALONG WITH IT